CAMBRIDGE
UNIVERSITY PRESS

Cambridge Lower Secondary
English

LEARNER'S BOOK 9

Graham Elsdon

CAMBRIDGE
UNIVERSITY PRESS

University Printing House, Cambridge CB2 8BS, United Kingdom

One Liberty Plaza, 20th Floor, New York, NY 10006, USA

477 Williamstown Road, Port Melbourne, VIC 3207, Australia

314–321, 3rd Floor, Plot 3, Splendor Forum, Jasola District Centre, New Delhi – 110025, India

103 Penang Road, #05-06/07, Visioncrest Commercial, Singapore 238467

Cambridge University Press is part of the University of Cambridge.

It furthers the University's mission by disseminating knowledge in the pursuit of education, learning and research at the highest international levels of excellence.

www.cambridge.org
Information on this title: www.cambridge.org/9781108746663

First published 2014
Second edition 2021

20 19 18 17 16 15 14 13

Printed in Dubai by Oriental Press

A catalogue record for this publication is available from the British Library

ISBN 978-1-108-74666-3 Paperback with Digital Access (1 Year)
ISBN 978-1-108-74667-0 Digital Learner's Book (1 Year)
ISBN 978-1-108-74668-7 eBook

....

> Introduction

Welcome to Stage 9 of Cambridge Lower Secondary English.

We are delighted to introduce you to a variety of fiction, non-fiction, poetry and drama texts, all of which have been selected to appeal to readers of your age. You will encounter texts from different countries and time periods, extend your English skills and develop your knowledge of literature.

You will read a dramatic tale set below the streets of Paris, perform your own drama scene and write a speech about an issue you feel strongly about. You will study thought-provoking poems about the passing of time, read about lost tribes and analyse a science-fiction story about a strange journey.

There are two complete short stories in this book. The first one, 'The Red-Headed League', is a mystery story featuring Sherlock Holmes. The second, 'The Journey Within', is a fantasy tale about a girl discovering her inner strength. Both of these stories will help you to understand structural patterns, and allow you to explore themes in a very detailed way.

We hope you will enjoy writing stories in a variety of genres, such as mystery and fantasy, as well as practising your persuasive and analytical skills. There are opportunities to create drama scenes, write poetry and refine your ability to use language in expressive and impactful ways.

You will have many opportunities to work in groups and pairs, exploring reactions to texts and issues affecting the world we live in. The projects at the end of each unit are designed to help develop the skills you have acquired, and allow you to practise the key skills of research and presentation that are essential for future study and work.

Reflecting on your own learning is an essential part of your development, so make use of the assessment and reflection features. They will allow you to see just how much progress you are making and help you to become a thoughtful and independent learner.

Good luck on the next stage of your learning journey.

Graham Elsdon

Contents

Contents

Writing	Speaking/Listening	Language focus	21st-century skills
Writing contemporary fantasy; writing a formal review; writing a drama scene; producing travel writing	Discussion work; reading prose and drama aloud; listening to and discussing opinions	Punctuation for rhetorical effect; extended metaphors	Creativity; collaboration
Summarising views; using colons and semi-colons; note taking; writing descriptively; making deductions; analysing character	Discussion work; performing a scene; listening to and discussing opinions;	Combining sentence types for effect; colons and semi-colons	Critical thinking; communication
Comparing characters; analysing structure; writing a report; writing a story ending; descriptive writing	Discussion work; improvising a conversation; listening to a playscript; dialogue reading	Working out the meaning of unfamiliar words; different types of imagery	Collaboration; creativity
Writing different types of poems; personal response; writing a speech; writing a story opening; writing a new chapter; making predictions	Discussion work; giving a speech; listening to an account	Tenses, conditionals and modals; verb choices	Creativity; critical thinking
Analysing dramatic structure; exploring contrast; writing a comedy scene; summarising structural patterns; imaginative writing; note taking; personal response; writing a discursive response	Discussion work; reading and performing a play; listening to an account	Asides and dramatic irony; layers of meaning in figurative language	Social responsibility; collaboration
Analysing a poem; describing the natural world; analysing spatial metaphors; writing sonnet lines; homecoming writing	Discussion work; exploring opinions; listening to thoughts and feeling	Rhyming couplets and imperfect rhyme; pathetic fallacy	Critical thinking; learning to learn
Writing a short fantasy account; analysing formality; describing a fantasy setting; imaginative monologue; analysing theme; writing a fantasy story	Discussion work; reading in dialogue parts; exploring and giving opinions	Motifs; levels of formality	Social responsibility; creativity
Note taking; analysis of language; writing a dramatic scene; writing a feature article; writing a persuasive speech; writing part of a science-fiction story	Discussion work; performing a scene; exploring agreement and disagreement; listening to personal accounts; giving a speech	Dramatic conflict via language; pronoun choices	Learning to learn; communication
Poetry analysis; translation of Shakespearean English; summarising; note taking; adapting *Macbeth*; writing biography; writing a feature article; writing a final scene; writing a short story with a twist	Discussion work; reading soliloquy; listening to account of genre	Ambiguous endings; puns and double meanings	Creativity; collaboration

> How to use this book

This book contains lots of different features that will help your learning. These are explained below.

This list sets out what you will learn in each session. You can use these points to identify the important topics for the lesson.

> **In this session, you will:**
> - explore the effect of structure and language choices
> - consider how punctuation choices can be used to present a character
> - write the continuation of a story in the style of an author.

This contains questions or activities to help find out what you know already about the topics in this session.

> **Getting started**
>
> In pairs, discuss mysterious characters from books and films that you know. What makes them seem mysterious and how do you react to them?

Important words are highlighted in the text when they first appear in the book. You will find an explanation of the meaning of these words in the margin. You will also find definitions of all these words in the glossary at the back of this book.

> **Key words**
>
> **sequence:** the order of events in a story
> **voice:** the way a particular character speaks or thinks in fiction, or the writer's tone and point of view in non-fiction

Activities give you the opportunity to practise and develop the skills that you learn in each session. Activities will involve answering questions or completing tasks. This includes listening activities where you hear a sound recording. These recordings can be played from the Digital edition of the Learner's Book. Your Digital edition also includes recordings of all the text extracts.

> 4 Most of the time, the writer addresses the reader using the plural **pronouns** 'we' and 'us'. This suggests that readers share his opinions about detective fiction.
>
> Write a brief analysis of the effect of this grammatical choice in the text. Why might the writer want to imply a link with the reader, and how is that related to the purpose of the text?
>
> 14 5 You are going to listen to some readers talking about detective fiction. As you listen, make notes on each reader's preferences and experiences of the genre. Then write a summary of these different views, explaining how each reader's experiences affect their opinions.

This will provide you with explanations of important content relating to grammar and language.

> **Language focus**
>
> Remember that there are four main sentence types: **simple**, **compound**, **complex** and **compound-complex**. Writers choose and position different sentence types carefully to support their purpose. Look at the example below, where a compound sentence is followed by a complex sentence:
> - Humans rely on others and they benefit from cooperation. Although humans can sometimes be selfish, working together is essential for human survival.

Each tip will help you to develop a technique or skill connected to reading, writing, speaking or listening.

> **Listening tip**
>
> When listening to texts in which speakers explain and justify their ideas, stay alert for the detail of their answer. Often, speakers give several reasons for their opinions, so listen carefully to their full response to get a complete understanding.

After completing an activity, this provides you with the opportunity to either assess your own work or another learner's work.

Self-assessment

Review your contribution to the group discussion.

- How thoroughly did you explore the points raised?
- Which of your comments did you feel helped to develop the discussion most effectively?

This contains questions that ask you to look back at what you have covered and reflect on your learning.

- What were the challenges of synthesising information?
- What other methods of finding and recording information in several different texts could you use? How would these help you?

This list summarises the important skills that you have learnt in the session.

Summary checklist

- ☐ I can analyse the effect of structural choices in a piece of travel writing.
- ☐ I can discuss and give a personal response to themes and ideas across a text.
- ☐ I can write, evaluate and edit a piece of travel writing.

These questions look back at some of the content you learnt in each session in this unit. If you can answer these, you are ready to move on to the next unit.

Check your progress

Answer the following questions.

1 Using examples, describe some of the ways in which fiction stories can be structured.
2 Using examples, explain how punctuation can create effects such as tension or excitement.
3 'People's experiences and preferences affect the way they choose and respond to texts.' Explain what this means, using your own words.
4 Describe the different ways you can use your voice and gesture to convey character in a drama script.
5 Describe the purposes and intended effects of travel writing.

At the end of each unit, there is a group project that you can carry out with other learners. This will involve using some of the knowledge that you learnt during the unit. Your project might involve creating or producing something, or you might all solve a problem together.

Project

In detective stories, the main character can be a private investigator, someone working for the police or even a normal person.

In groups, you will research detective figures in fiction from around the world. You will explore how detectives are presented and what features they have in common.

As a group, make a list of detective figures in stories you have read. Then do some research into stories from a range of times and cultures. You could find out about detectives in adult fiction such as Auguste Dupin (the first detective character in literature), Bhaduri Moshai, Philip Marlowe, Mme Ramotswe or Miss Marple. Remember to look at detectives in children's literature too, such as the Diamond Brothers or Young Sherlock Holmes. Try to read some extracts from books that these characters feature in.

Next, explore the qualities and styles of these detectives. You could consider:

- gender – are there typical characteristics of female and male detectives?
- details of their personal lives – are they generally happy, satisfied people?
- attitudes to authority – do they follow rules or do they challenge authority?
- their motivations for fighting crime.

As you work in your group, allocate roles for your research. For example, one of you might focus on children's literature, or one of you may have detailed knowledge of the genre already and could be the 'expert adviser'.

Once you have discussed your findings as a group, prepare a five-minute presentation for the class.

Going underground

In this unit, you will read prose and play versions of a modern fiction text set in a mysterious place beneath a city. You will practise your drama and reviewing skills and will read and discuss a piece of travel writing.

> 1.1 Relic

In this session, you will:

- read a story opening and discuss genre
- explore how key information helps readers understand a character's actions
- consider the effect of story structure
- discuss and summarise your impressions of a story opening.

Getting started

What makes an exciting opening chapter in a story? In pairs, discuss your ideas and talk about some opening chapters in books that you have enjoyed.

Darkparis

In this session and the next, you are going to read the opening of a novel called *Darkparis*. The story is set in Paris. The main character, Louis, finds himself in the mysterious catacombs below the city streets, led by his new companion, Relic. Catacombs were originally mines that were later used as storage tunnels. The catacombs are a popular tourist attraction in Paris today.

Extract 1

Louis stood just inside the entrance, watching the shadows from the **flickering** torches dance on the walls. This was the first time he'd been inside the ancient catacombs and the situation felt unnatural. He could see Relic begin to make her way through the narrow tunnels, and despite his hesitation, something – he didn't know what – made him trust her. Somehow, she was the key to this. He started to follow her.

Darkparis. How did he end up here – and why?

He was bored. Bored with work, bored with home, bored with life. Louis was 17 years old and living in a small apartment in northern Paris. That much sounded like a dream, but Louis had soon discovered how dull life in the world beyond childhood could be. His job in the local supermarket hardly filled him with joy. Yes, he was bored. Lonely, actually. So when a dark-haired girl he'd never met before had approached him as he left work the previous day and asked him how to find the entrance to the catacombs, he was pleased to have a brief distraction.

'I'll show you,' he found himself saying. 'I'm heading that way.'

The girl smiled and introduced herself as she began walking alongside him. 'I'm Relic,' she said.

As they navigated the back streets of Paris, Louis found himself in an easy conversation with Relic. She had a kind face and seemed a little too **naïve** to live in the city. At the same time, though, there was something odd about her – as if she belonged to another time.

flickering: shining unsteadily
naïve: lacking experience or wisdom

They arrived at the catacombs quicker than he would have liked. 'Thanks, Louis,' Relic said, turning towards the entrance. And it flashed through Louis's mind that he had never told her his name. 'By the way, The Doorkeeper thinks you're the one. Be back here at nine o'clock tomorrow night.'

With that, she was gone.

But he knew he'd be there the following evening.

1   Which **genre** of **fiction** do you think *Darkparis* belongs to? Discuss your ideas in pairs. Consider:

- the title

- the names of the characters

- the **setting**

- the events of the story so far

- the picture below from the front cover of the book.

2   Writers often give **explicit information**, which helps readers to understand events as the story develops. In the first three paragraphs of *Darkparis*, you find out that Louis is bored and lonely, and that he likes Relic. Write a paragraph explaining:

- how this information helps you to understand and interpret Louis's decision at the end of the extract

- what you think might happen later in the story.

Key words

genre: a particular type of text – for example, adventure, comedy, crime, science fiction

fiction: stories about imaginary characters and events

setting: the location where a story takes place

Key words

explicit information: ideas and details that a writer states directly

3   The structure of a story affects how readers experience and understand it. For example, a writer makes deliberate choices about the order of events, how time is presented and when characters are introduced.

In pairs, discuss the following structural choices in *Darkparis* and the effect they have on the reader:

- the description of the catacombs in the opening sentences
- the use of **flashback** to show Louis's first meeting with Relic and his feelings about his life
- the mention of The Doorkeeper at the end of the extract.

4   In groups, discuss your reactions to the opening of *Darkparis*. Talk about:

- whether the story interested you and why
- what you thought of the structure
- whether or not you were interested in the two main characters.

Key word

flashback: a part of a story that goes back in time to explain an event

Self-assessment

Review your contribution to the group discussion.

- How thoroughly did you explore the points raised?
- Which of your comments did you feel helped to develop the discussion most effectively?

5   Write a summary of the different viewpoints expressed by members of your group. Structure your writing using a subheading for each of the three bullet points you discussed.

Speaking tip

It is important to make appropriate and well-judged contributions to a group discussion. That means always trying to develop the discussion. You can do this by building on a point that someone else has made, or by challenging something that has been said.

Summary checklist

- [ ] I can identify a fiction genre based on a story's key features.
- [ ] I understand how explicit information helps a reader understand a character's actions.
- [ ] I can comment on the effect of story structure.
- [ ] I can express my opinion of a story opening and summarise my own and others' ideas.

You do know there is no going back to your old life, don't you, Louis? You know you must prove yourself, don't you, Louis? I don't think you are weak, but I'm not yet sure if you are strong. Or strong enough, at least.'

A low mist was creeping into the tunnel.

'I'm not weak,' responded Louis, trying to hide the **quiver** in his voice.

'Let us see,' continued The Doorkeeper, his eyes **piercing** Louis. 'We define ourselves through the choices we make, even when the mist of indecision **lingers**.'

'Welcome to . . . The Test!' proclaimed The Doorkeeper.

There was a split second of inaction, and then . . .

They were off! Relic disappeared down one tunnel and The Doorkeeper down another. The third tunnel stood there, beckoning Louis.

He was deep in Darkparis; buried in the catacombs, with their foul-smelling passageways and strange mist.

Which way now? Go on or go home?

> **quiver:** a shake
> **piercing:** cutting through
> **lingers:** hangs around

1 In this extract, the writer tells the story in **chronological order**. The effect of this is to focus on the present action in the catacombs, to develop the reader's understanding of situation and character.

Copy and complete the following table to show the effect of other structural choices in this extract.

Structural choice	Effect
Focusing on the setting in the first three paragraphs	
Making The Doorkeeper more central	
Using **dialogue** to show the interaction between Louis and The Doorkeeper	
Ending on a **cliffhanger**	

Key words

chronological order: the order in which events occur by time

dialogue: conversation between two or more people or characters, written as direct speech

cliffhanger: a dramatic ending which leaves the reader in suspense

2   Writers choose language carefully to support their purpose and the effect they are trying to achieve. In pairs, analyse how the following language choices create a sense of mystery:

   a   **aural**, **olfactory** and **visual images** such as *rebounded off the walls*, *foul-smelling passageways* and *flaming torches*

   b   the use of **symbols** such as The Fork and the mist

   c   the use of **antithesis** in The Doorkeeper's dialogue (for example, *a world that <u>few</u> see, but a world which sees <u>many</u>*).

Language focus

Punctuation can be used for rhetorical purposes. This means that punctuation marks such as question marks, exclamation marks and **ellipses** can shape an argument or suggest something about a character or situation.

A question mark can be used to signal a **rhetorical question**. It can also create a variety of **tones**, such as making a speaker sound slightly threatening or surprised ('Why on earth did you make that choice?').

Exclamation marks can also create different effects, such as excitement ('Welcome to your new life!') or anger ('I insist you leave now!').

Ellipses may suggest a variety of emotions or moods, such as nervousness/hesitation ('Please . . . can I leave now?') or a sense of drama ('And now . . . here it is!').

3   The Doorkeeper is presented as an unusual, powerful character. One method the writer uses to achieve this is punctuation choices in The Doorkeeper's dialogue. For example, the exclamation mark in *And so young Louis visits us again!* conveys the confidence and volume of the character's voice.

   In pairs, discuss what the following punctuation choices suggest about The Doorkeeper.

   a   the use of question marks in phrases such as *You do know there is no going back to your old life, don't you, Louis?*

   b   the ellipsis in *Welcome to . . . The Test!*

Key words

aural image: an image that appeals to the sense of hearing

olfactory image: an image that appeals to the sense of smell

visual image: an image that appeals to the sense of sight

symbol: a literal object that stands for or represents something else

antithesis: the use of opposites or contrasting ideas

ellipsis: a set of three dots (. . .) used to indicate that words have been left out, or to mark a pause in speech

rhetorical question: a question designed to make a point rather than expecting an answer

tone: the way that someone speaks or how a piece of writing sounds, which helps suggest mood and feelings

4   Look at the following notes, which the writer made when planning the next part of the story.

Louis follows The Doorkeeper. After travelling through a dark, winding tunnel, he catches up with The Doorkeeper, who advises him to turn back and follow his own path. When he arrives back at The Fork, he takes the third tunnel. It leads him to a huge maze.

Using these notes, write the next part of *Darkparis*. Write in the same style as the extracts you have read, using similar language and structural techniques. For example, you could use a chronological **sequence** or a flashback. Use punctuation and other language techniques, such as antithesis, to present the **voice** of The Doorkeeper.

Start by deciding whether you want to develop the writer's plan. Write 200 words, making sure your spelling is accurate and your handwriting is fluent.

Peer assessment

In pairs, read your stories aloud. Give your partner feedback on the effectiveness of their language and structural choices. Comment on:

- how similar the language choices are to those used in *Darkparis*
- the sequence of the story – did it help to maintain your interest?

Summary checklist

☐ I can analyse the effect of a writer's structural and language choices.

☐ I can comment on how punctuation choices help to create a distinctive character.

☐ I can use specific language, structural and grammatical techniques to write in the style of another author.

Key words

sequence: the order of events in a story

voice: the way a particular character speaks or thinks in fiction, or the writer's tone and point of view in non-fiction

Writing tip

Planning before you write can be useful, but remember that ideas may come to you as you write, so you may only need a basic plan. Be confident in deciding how much planning you need to do based on the amount of time you have and your writing skills.

> 1.3 Reviewing *Darkparis*

In this session, you will:

- make some book recommendations
- explore how personal context affects the reading and writing of texts
- synthesise information from different sources
- write a formal review.

Getting started

In pairs, make a quick list of books you have read and enjoyed recently. Then discuss:

- why you chose those books
- whether the settings in the books were similar or different to the world you live in.

1 People often ask for or offer recommendations for books to read. When suggesting a book to a friend, it is useful to know what genres and types of text they like. In groups, share your ideas from the Getting started activity, then make some recommendations for books you think other group members would enjoy.

People's personal experiences and preferences affect the way they choose and respond to texts. A reader's personal **context** – their background and beliefs – can also lead them to interpret stories in different ways. Consider the readers' reactions to the first few chapters of *Darkparis* on the next page.

Key word

context: the situation within which something exists or happens

> 1.2 The Doorkeeper

In this session, you will:

- explore the effect of structure and language choices
- consider how punctuation choices can be used to present a character
- write the continuation of a story in the style of an author.

Getting started

In pairs, discuss mysterious characters from books and films that you know. What makes them seem mysterious and how do you react to them?

Read another extract from *Darkparis*.

02

Extract 2

And so here he was, in Darkparis, following Relic through the tunnels. They seemed to shift . . . was that real, or just an effect caused by the flaming torches and low ceilings?

It wasn't long before they came to The Fork, where the tunnel split three ways. There, in the yellow light from the torch flames, stood The Doorkeeper. As he spoke, his words **rebounded** off the walls.

'And so young Louis visits us!' he declared. 'And what is he discovering I wonder? He is discovering Darkparis – a world that few see, but a world which sees many!'

Louis and Relic said nothing, and the silence was filled with the unpleasant sound of an animal **scurrying** along the tunnel.

'Paris is for the fearful,' boomed The Doorkeeper, 'But Darkparis is for the fearless.

rebounded: bounced back

scurrying: moving quickly with short steps

Ayesha, 14

I enjoyed this. I like books with mysterious characters and strange settings, mainly because they seem very different to normal life. For me, reading is a chance to escape reality, so I enjoyed reading about the character of The Doorkeeper because he seems powerful and mysterious at the same time. I like characters who have some type of secret knowledge. In comparison, Louis seems dull and a bit disappointing as a character. I'd like to read a bit more of this book to find out what happens and why The Doorkeeper is testing Louis. I think this is a story about how people don't realise that there are ways of living differently to their own.

Vanessa, 13

I thought Darkparis was okay. The best bit about it was the character of Relic. She seemed to be intriguing, not only to Louis, but to the reader. There were lots of unanswered questions about her, so I'd like to know who she is and how she develops in the full novel. I like novels with strong female characters, mainly because these days I think girls can do anything that boys can. That's why I usually choose books where the main character is a girl. I found the opening of Darkparis disappointing because Relic doesn't really feature much — it's mainly about male characters.

Alexei, 18

This is the type of book I would have read a few years ago and enjoyed. At that age, I used to like books set in underground places. Now that I'm older, it didn't appeal as much, but it did have interesting characters. The character I most identified with was Louis. I know how it feels to be bored. I live in a small village in Russia and would like a more exciting life! The other thing I liked was the setting. Last year, my family went on holiday to Paris and I visited the catacombs, so I could imagine the setting of this book. It's fun to read books set in places you know.

2 Answer the following questions.

    a What type of texts does Ayesha prefer, and how has this influenced her reaction to *Darkparis*?

    b Explain why Vanessa has a slightly negative reaction to the novel.

    c Alexei has mixed views about the novel. What factors have informed his reactions?

3 Stories – even ones set in unusual locations – may reflect the experiences and values of the writer. You are going to listen to the author of *Darkparis* discussing why she wrote the book. As you listen, make notes on:

    • why she chose the setting

    • why she chose Louis as a central character

    • what she says about the message of her book.

Think about the best way to record your notes so they will be clear when you refer back to them later.

Listening tip

When listening to texts in which speakers explain and justify their ideas, stay alert for the detail of their answer. Often, speakers give several reasons for their opinions, so listen carefully to their full response to get a complete understanding.

---

4 Synthesising information means combining details from different sources, usually to find links and make an overall point. To do this, you need to be able to locate, track and **summarise** particular information.

Look at the following comment about *Darkparis*: 'Louis is a character who appeals to all readers.' Is this an accurate statement? Begin by looking through the notes you made on the views of Ayesha, Vanessa and Alexei. Use reading strategies such as **skimming** and **scanning** to locate relevant information. Make notes as you go, then in small groups discuss these ideas as well as your own views and decide whether or not Louis appeals to all readers.

Key words

summarise: to explain the main points of a text in a few words

skimming: reading a text quickly to get the overall idea

scanning: looking through a text quickly to find particular details

- What were the challenges of synthesising information?
- What other methods of finding and recording information in several different texts could you use? How would these help you?

5 Imagine that you are a professional book reviewer whose job is to advise companies whether or not a book should be published. A book company has asked you to write a formal review of the opening chapters of *Darkparis*. You should give your own views and any others you have encountered in this session. Your review should comment on:

- the choice of the characters and settings
- the appeal of the storyline
- whether the novel is likely to be popular with 12–18-year-olds.

Your audience is the head of children's books at the book company. Use **formal language** and **standard English**. Read some formal online book reviews to see how they are written and to get some ideas for extending your own vocabulary and language. Use features of review writing such as subheadings and bullet points where appropriate. Write 250 words.

Summary checklist

☐ I can listen to the type of books people are interested in and make some recommendations.
☐ I understand how personal context influences writers' choices and readers' reactions to a text.
☐ I can use different strategies to synthesise information from a range of sources.
☐ I can write a formal review using standard English.

Reading tip

When reading multiple texts, use techniques such as scanning to locate key information and then read this closely to interpret the details. Use a table or other visual layout to record the information so you can see similarities and differences next to each other.

Key words

formal language: the form of English used in more 'serious' texts and situations, such as news reports or official speeches

standard English: the most widely accepted form of English that is not specific to a particular region

> 1.4 The second test

Getting started

In how many ways can you use your voice to convey power? In pairs, practise different ways of delivering the line 'What's this about? I want to leave!' Vary the volume and pace of your delivery.

Key word

pace: the speed at which someone speaks or how quickly events take place in a story

Darkparis: The play

Read the following scene from the play version of *Darkparis*. It takes place after Louis has completed his first test, in which he entered the third tunnel and found his way through a maze.

Scene 4: The Second Test

The scene takes place in a large, cave-like underground area, lit with flaming torches. There are two people in the shadows at the back of the stage. The sound of rushing water can be heard. LOUIS *emerges from a tunnel.*

| THE DOORKEEPER | Well done, young Louis. You completed the Moving Maze. Not many do. Well, not alive anyway. |

LOUIS *looks up at* THE DOORKEEPER.

| LOUIS | What's this about? I want to leave! |

Pause.

| THE DOORKEEPER | We both know you can't. You chose the third tunnel, Louis. You *chose* your own route. You chose. Why was that, Louis? |

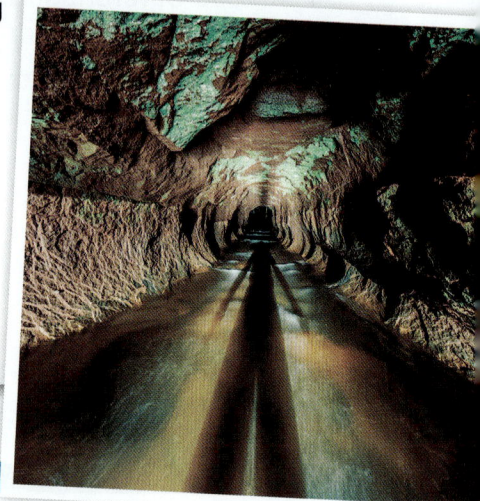

LOUIS *gets to his feet.*

LOUIS I don't know.

THE DOORKEEPER You followed your instincts. Trusted yourself . . . the sign of a strong person. You are strong.

Pause.

THE DOORKEEPER Now prove yourself in your next choice.

The rear of the stage lights up. We can see RELIC, *suspended above a fast-moving river. She is* gagged. *There is also an* OLD MAN *standing very still. He is looking into a glass ball.*

OLD MAN (*to* LOUIS) There you are, master Louis – at school. And you're unhappy. Deeply unhappy. Something happened. Bad choices – but they weren't your choices to make. And now you're in a supermarket. You're unhappy there, too. You want more . . . you want a new life.

THE DOORKEEPER This is why you're here, Louis. To prove yourself through the choices you make. To choose your new life.

THE DOORKEEPER *takes off* RELIC's *gag. The river below her crashes along.*

RELIC Help me, Louis! Help me! Don't let me die! Please!

LOUIS *looks confused.*

THE DOORKEEPER Listen to her, Louis. Listen.

RELIC You've got to help me! If I go in the river, I die. You can't let me die. That river only flows one way, and there is no return.

LOUIS What do I need to do?

OLD MAN It's you or her.

Pause.

THE DOORKEEPER One of you enters the river. It's you or her. You choose.

RELIC Please, Louis!

THE DOORKEEPER Time to choose, young man.

LOUIS (*to* THE DOORKEEPER) I have. I refuse.

gagged: having a covering over the mouth so someone cannot speak

1   In groups of four, read the scene aloud, taking one speaking part each. You do not need to act it out, just concentrate on reading the words accurately and understanding what is happening.

2   This scene explores the **theme** of power. The Doorkeeper and the Old Man have power over Louis. Relic seems completely powerless and so does Louis, although in the last line he seems to be challenging The Doorkeeper.

In your groups, discuss how you could perform this scene to highlight the theme of power. The **script** does not give any ideas about tone of voice, **gesture** or movement, so start by considering how you might speak your lines to show your character's power.

Perform the scene, using a range of movement and gesture appropriate to your character.

Key words

theme: the main subject of a talk, book, film, poem, etc.

script: the words and actions from a play written down for the actors to use

gesture: movements of the hands or arms to add emphasis or bring a story to life

Speaking tip

Use the range of your voice to create a strong sense of drama. Actors vary the volume, tone and pace of the voice throughout a performance. It is this variety that helps to show the emotions of the character they are playing and to maintain the audience's interest.

Peer assessment

Give some feedback to another member of your group.
* How well did they use the range of their voice?
* How convincingly did their movements and gestures convey their character's power?

3   Look back at this scene and at the **prose** chapters (Extracts 1 and 2). In pairs, discuss the theme of power in these texts, exploring how Louis develops from a powerless character to one who has power. Find examples to support your ideas and sustain the discussion by talking about them in depth.

4   Playwrights decide the order of events and the information they reveal to the audience at different points in a scene. They do this to create different effects, such as establishing a **mood** of mystery or tension.

Key words

prose: the form of language found in novels and non-fiction texts such as articles, written in paragraphs rather than verse

mood: the feeling created by the words, sounds and images in a text

Here are three structural choices the writer has made in this scene:

- At the start of the scene, the audience can see two people at the back of the stage (but they cannot see who they are) and can hear the sound of water.

- In the middle of the scene, a new character – the Old Man – is introduced.

- At the end, Louis challenges The Doorkeeper's authority, creating a cliffhanger.

What effect do each of these choices have on you as a reader? Write a brief explanation of how you react at each point.

5 Write the next scene of the play. Start by thinking about the structure:

- What will happen between Louis and The Doorkeeper?

- How will Relic's problem be resolved?

- Will the Old Man play a more important role?

- Will you introduce a new character?

- Will you end the scene with another cliffhanger?

Try experimenting with the order of events and the content of the scene. You are writing for teenagers who enjoy mysterious, dramatic fiction, so make sure your scene will appeal to them.

When you write the words for each character, maintain their voice and personality from the scene you have read. Your finished scene should be 250 words.

> **Writing tip**
>
> Always begin scriptwriting by planning the sequence of events. Think about the large blocks of the story – what happens and in what order. Before you start to write, you should know how the scene will end.

Summary checklist

- ☐ I can use voice and gesture to convey character and emotion in a dramatic performance.
- ☐ I can analyse how a theme is presented and developed in different texts.
- ☐ I can comment on the effect of different structural choices in a script.
- ☐ I can write a dramatic scene, maintaining the voice and personality of the characters.

> 1.5 Visiting Coober Pedy

In this session, you will:

- explore the implications of explicit information
- consider how extended metaphors contribute to the purpose and effect of a text
- analyse a writer's language choices.

Getting started

In pairs, describe an interesting place you have visited. Explain what made it memorable – was it the people, the buildings or an unusual event?

Coober Pedy

Travel writing is a **non-fiction** genre in which the writer describes a place they have visited. The purpose of travel writing is mainly to entertain the reader by describing interesting locations and people. But travel writing is also meant to make the reader think and reflect upon different lifestyles and human experiences.

The following article describes a visit to Coober Pedy, a town in Australia where most of the people live under the ground.

Key word

non-fiction: writing that is about real events and facts

Extract 1

Coober Pedy: Getting below the surface

I spent three days travelling to Coober Pedy. The nearest town is 400 miles away, there's no wi-fi, and I've just spent the night sleeping in what is effectively a hole in the ground. When I decided to be a travel writer, I was expecting something much more glamorous than this . . .

Coober Pedy is in the middle of the South Australian desert. It's 1800 miles from Canberra, Australia's capital city, but it might as well be on Mars. As you approach by car, your vision is filled with **otherworldly** images: the long stretches of dusty red landscape, strange hills of white soil and randomly scattered mining holes make this place look like something from science fiction. It's a little bit **unnerving**.

The weather is otherworldly too. Summers are hotter than the sun and the winters are colder than Mars. That's why most of the townspeople live under the ground in dugouts, trying to make a living in this place of extremes. People started coming here in the 1920s, attracted by the precious **opals** to be found buried here. They sought their riches by **blasting** and digging their way through the rocks in a desperate attempt to get rich quick. The harsh surroundings were just something they had to put up with. Living below the surface was the best option.

When I first arrived in the town, it struck me just how unreal the whole place seemed – like a deserted film set for a Martian movie where I was the unwilling heroine. The red dust and mine shafts of this new reality didn't seem real at all.

But it did make for some nice photos.

otherworldly: relating to a strange, alternative world

unnerving: causing a loss of confidence

opal: a precious stone

blasting: blowing up or breaking apart

1   In pairs, discuss:

   a   what the writer states about the area and what is being implied about Coober Pedy

   b   your initial impression of the writer's voice and attitude.

2   The writer explicitly mentions how long it takes to reach Coober Pedy and the reason why people settled there in the 1920s. What effect does this have on your impressions of the town and its inhabitants? Discuss your ideas in small groups.

Language focus

Writers often make comparisons to help readers picture or understand a topic. Literary techniques such as **simile** and **metaphor** are particularly effective ways of making comparisons, and writers may repeat and develop a comparison throughout a text as an **extended metaphor**. Look at this example from a piece of travel writing. The writer uses water-based comparisons to show the heat of a desert town:

- The haze of heat distorted Mandora, making the town look like it was under water. In the dazzling light, the shape of human bodies seemed to shift as waves of heat rippled. People swam slowly towards me, their limbs flailing and their faces made wide by the watery midday world.

Notice how the references to water and swimming contribute to the overall purpose of the description. The comparison shows the reader clearly how hot it is in the desert, as well as how the power of nature can alter the way we perceive our surroundings.

Key words

simile: a type of figurative language in which one thing is compared to something else using the words 'as' or 'like'

metaphor: a type of comparison that describes one thing as if it is something else

extended metaphor: a metaphor that is used, repeated and developed in a piece of writing

---

3   The writer makes language choices to present Coober Pedy as an unusual place. Write a 100-word paragraph analysing the use and overall impact of the comparisons with Mars in the article. Be precise and perceptive in your analysis. Choose quotations carefully to support your ideas.

4   Read the following example response to Activity 3.
In pairs, discuss what makes it perceptive.

By referring to the 'long stretches of dusty red landscape' and
'a deserted film set for a Martian movie', the writer not only
describes the physical appearance of the town, she also shows
that it is so unusual that it could be on another planet. The
implication is that Coober Pedy seems alien — as if it is not
normal. The writer implies that Coober Pedy is out of touch
and perhaps empty, and suggests that she does not really want
to stay there. There is a sense that the writer thinks the
town and its people are strange.

Self-assessment

Reread your own paragraph from Activity 3.

- How effective is it compared to the example response in Activity 4?

- How could you improve your answer?

Summary checklist

- [ ] I can identify explicit information and comment on its implications in a travel article.
- [ ] I can explain how imagery, including extended metaphors, can be used for purpose and effect.
- [ ] I can analyse the effect of a writer's language choices precisely and perceptively.

> 1.6 Living under the ground

In this session, you will:

- explore the effect of structural choices in travel writing
- discuss and give a personal response to themes and ideas
- produce and edit a piece of travel writing.

Getting started

What is your impression of Coober Pedy so far? Would you like to visit it or even live there? Explain your views to a partner.

Read the next part of the article about Coober Pedy. Here, the writer meets Alinta, one of the town's inhabitants. Notice how the writer has structured the article so that this conversation comes after the description of the town (Extract 1 in Session 1.5).

Extract 2

Alinta rolls her eyes when I ask her how she manages to live here. She's a bright-eyed, funny 17-year-old who has big plans for the future. For now, she tells me, she's helping to run her parents' small tourist dugout, but next year, she's going to Melbourne to study computing.

'It's all normal to me,' she says. 'It's not like we're living at the Earth's core. We've got electricity, you know!' She says this comically, but I suspect she gets a bit tired of outsiders like me assuming that the people of Coober Pedy are a long way **behind the times**.

The family's electricity comes partly from diesel and partly from solar power, but as it turns out, the diesel is expensive, so they need income from tourists. It seems to me that Alinta and her family must have to be careful with the way they use electricity, and also live in hope that enough curious travellers decide to visit.

> **behind the times:** not modern; stuck in the past

They do seem an **inventive** family, making the best of the resources they have, but still I wonder how long they can last.

The town feels like it is living in the past rather than looking to its future. The main appeal for tourists is Coober Pedy's mining history, but there's only so much interest there. What will the Coober Pedy of 2060 look like? Is it possible for humans to continue to live in such extreme landscapes?

The journey back to Canberra was long. I felt exhausted as I sat in my modern apartment looking through photos of the red landscape and tried to write this article. The **drone** of traffic and the continuous **pinging** of my phone seemed alien to me now and made me wonder if a life under the ground wasn't such a bad idea after all.

inventive: creative
drone: a low sound
pinging: making a short high-pitched sound

1   Why do you think the writer introduces Alinta at this point in the article? How does the interview with her change your impression of life in Coober Pedy? Discuss your ideas in pairs.

2   The concluding paragraphs are a key structural feature of travel writing. This is where a writer usually reflects on what they have learnt from their travels.

In your pairs, explore the effect of the last part of this article, including:

*   the writer's feelings about Coober Pedy

*   how she feels as she returns to her room

*   the effect that the last paragraph of the article has on you – how do you react to the author's final judgement about Coober Pedy?

3 Good travel writing gets a reader thinking about broader issues.
For example, this article shows that:

- there are many different ways of living, and they all have good
  and bad points

- it is difficult to live without modern facilities

- people who live privileged lives often look down on others

- wherever they live, most people have the same feelings and
  ambitions

- modern living is destroying old ways of living.

In pairs, use the prompts above to discuss what you have read,
choosing language carefully to express your ideas. At the end of
your discussion, sum up your personal response to the ideas in
the article.

4 You are now going to produce a piece of travel writing describing a
visit either to the underground town of Matmata in Tunisia or to a
place you have visited yourself that you would like to write about.
You should write around 300 words.

If you want to write about Matmata, you can use the following
facts and pictures to help you. You could also do some independent
research. If you are writing about a place you have really visited,
start by creating a fact file of your own like the one below.

> **Matmata fact file**
> - There are around 2000 people living in Matmata.
> - They live in houses that are formed by making a
>   large pit in the ground and then creating linked
>   underground rooms.
> - Most of the people living there rely on money
>   from tourism.
> - The town was used as a location in the film
>   *Star Wars: A New Hope*.

> **Reading tip**
>
> Giving a personal
> response means
> thinking about
> how a piece
> of writing
> has affected
> you. Start by
> considering
> your emotional
> response – for
> example, does
> the text make you
> feel pity, anger,
> joy or sadness?

Think about the structure of your writing. You could start by describing the journey, then meeting a local person and then end by reflecting on your experience. The voice you use and the viewpoint you express are also important. What attitude will you adopt? Make suitable language choices and use techniques such as metaphor where appropriate.

Peer assessment

Swap articles from Activity 4 with a partner and give them feedback.

- How effectively is their article organised – does it have a clear structure?
- How effective are their language choices – do they help you picture the town?

5 Edit your article before creating your final draft. Think carefully about the effectiveness of your language and structural choices. Make changes that will achieve your overall purpose.

Summary checklist

☐ I can analyse the effect of structural choices in a piece of travel writing.

☐ I can discuss and give a personal response to themes and ideas across a text.

☐ I can write, evaluate and edit a piece of travel writing.

Check your progress

Answer the following questions.

1   Using examples, describe some of the ways in which fiction stories can be structured.

2   Using examples, explain how punctuation can create effects such as tension or excitement.

3   'People's experiences and preferences affect the way they choose and respond to texts.' Explain what this means, using your own words.

4   Describe the different ways you can use your voice and gesture to convey character in a drama script.

5   Describe the purposes and intended effects of travel writing.

6   Explain some features of effective travel writing.

Project

Humans are fascinated by what happens below ground. Many stories and films are set below the earth or feature characters who live underground.

In groups, you are going to make a collection of fictional texts that feature aspects of underground life. For example, you might explore novels such as the Middle-Earth books by J. R. R. Tolkien, *Neverwhere* by Neil Gaiman and *Artemis Fowl* by Eoin Colfer. There are many Marvel comics and films, such as *Journey to the Centre of the Earth* and *How to Train Your Dragon*, which also use underground settings.

Once you have read and researched these and other texts, work as a group to discuss them and choose the most interesting or descriptive passages from them. Then, prepare a presentation for your class in which you discuss these texts. In your presentation, you should:

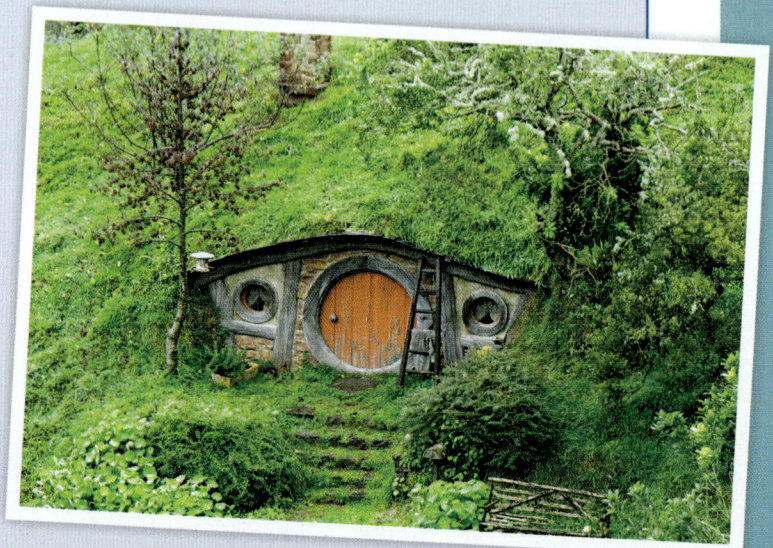

*   introduce the texts you have chosen

*   read some passages from the texts about life underground

*   analyse why these texts appeal to readers.

Your presentation should last ten minutes and should feature visual aids if appropriate.

2 Law and order

In this unit, you will read an account of how people understand right from wrong, and will read texts about various real-life investigators. You will also explore an extract from a detective novel and consider why many readers enjoy this kind of fiction.

> 2.1 Right and wrong

In this session, you will:

- consider the implications of key information in an explanatory text
- explore the effects of different sentence types
- compare language, purpose and context in related texts.

Getting started

In pairs, discuss times when you have felt guilty about something you have – or have not – done. Why might guilt be a useful emotion for us to feel?

Understanding right and wrong

Read the following extract from a book aimed at learners at secondary school. It explains how humans understand right from wrong.

The importance of conscience

Feeling the difference between right and wrong

A conscience is like a voice in your head that tells you whether your actions are good or bad. It's not actually a voice, of course. It's your emotions. Emotions are powerful feelings, and although emotions can be positive things, such as joy, **empathy** and **compassion**, it is negative emotions that warn us about our thoughts and actions. For instance, have you ever felt guilt, shame or a fear of how others might judge you? It is these negative feelings that tell humans to stop what they are doing, or to think carefully before they act. But how did humans develop a conscience?

Human needs

Humans are social beings. We live in groups and work together to get things done. We help each other, not just because we're kind, but because we need each other in order to survive. Since ancient times, we have learnt that if we **cooperate**, life is easier and better, and we have also learnt that when we help someone, we are rewarded. Humans are very good at remembering who has helped us, and who hasn't. We like those who help. We don't like selfish people.

When we do good things, we feel good. If we share and help, we feel positive emotions. If we don't cooperate or if we cause problems, we feel guilt and embarrassment. It is these feelings – or **anticipation** of these feelings – that are what we call a conscience.

Brain networks

Scientists have discovered that three different networks of the brain contribute to our conscience. The first is concerned with understanding other people – the ability to imagine what others are thinking. The second network is connected with pain. Understanding the pain of others helps us to empathise with people's feelings. Finally, the decision-making network in our brain helps us to judge what is the right course of action. This network balances our needs with the feelings of others and tells us what to do.

empathy: the ability to understand and share the feelings of others

compassion: concern and pity for others

cooperate: work together

anticipation: the feeling of expecting something to happen

1   The writer says: *It is these negative feelings that tell humans to stop what they are doing, or to think carefully before they act.*

Make brief notes on:

- what this statement means

- how it links to the ideas and explanations shown in the rest of the article.

Language focus

Remember that there are four main sentence types: **simple**, **compound**, **complex** and **compound-complex**. Writers choose and position different sentence types carefully to support their purpose. Look at the example below, where a compound sentence is followed by a complex sentence:

- Humans rely on others and they benefit from cooperation. Although humans can sometimes be selfish, working together is essential for human survival.

The first sentence provides key facts for the reader to focus on, then the second sentence develops and extends the point, providing an explanation. Together, they help the reader understand the point and convey the information in a gradual way.

Now look at this example, in which a compound-complex sentence is followed by a simple sentence:

- Although humans can sometimes be selfish, working together is important for human survival and also for social well-being. Cooperation between humans is essential.

Here, the detail is given in the first sentence and the second sentence reinforces the main point. The effect of this is to sum up and direct the reader to the overall message in the text.

Key words

simple sentence: a sentence with one main clause

compound sentence: a sentence with two main clauses joined by 'and', 'but', 'or'

complex sentence: a sentence with one main clause and one or more dependent clauses

compound-complex sentence: a sentence containing a compound sentence that also has one or more subordinate clauses

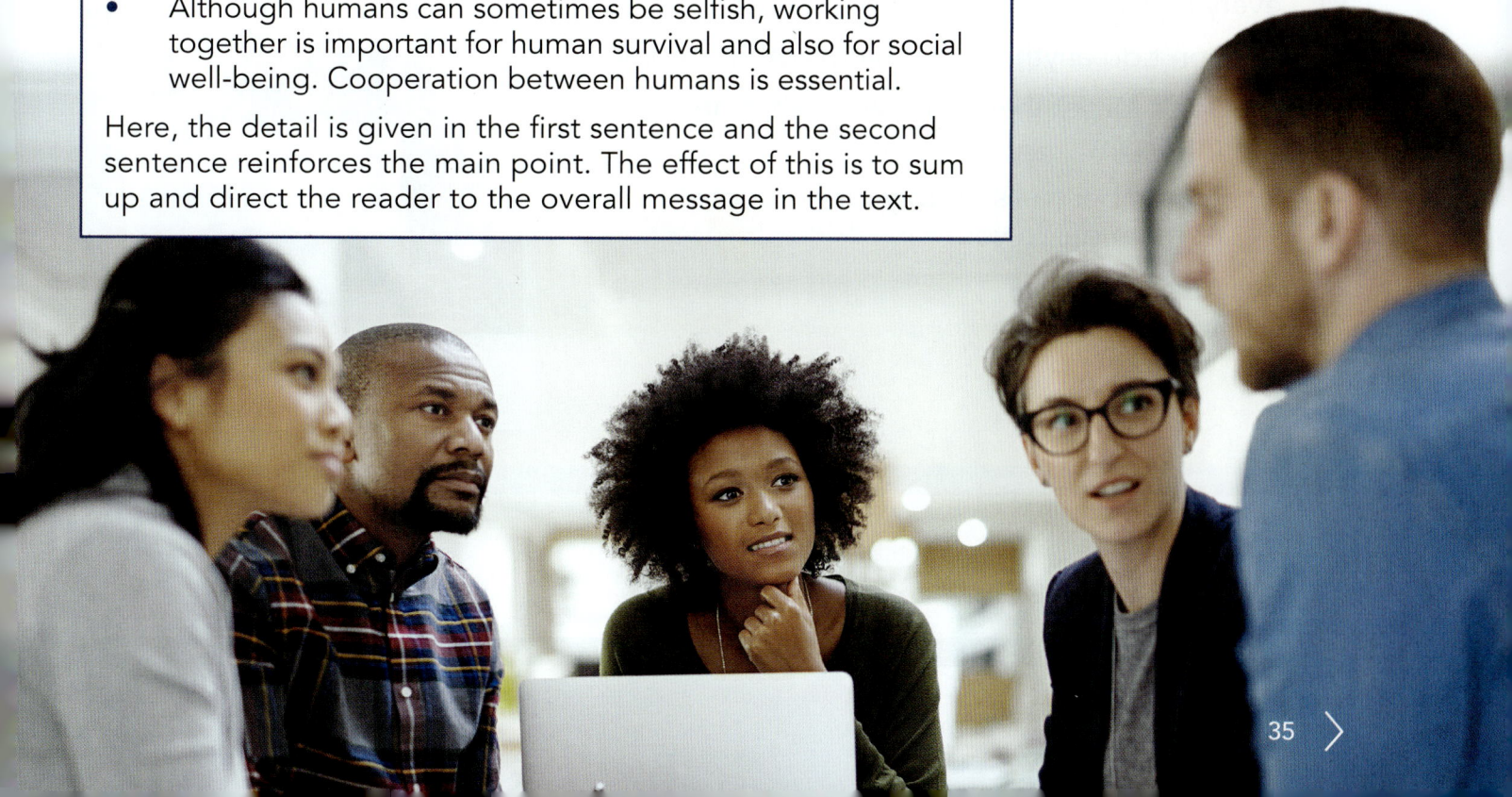

2   Reread 'The importance of conscience'. What is the effect of the different sentence combinations the writer has used? Choose two examples and write a paragraph explaining how it helps the purpose of the article.

3   Here is an extract from another text on the same topic. This comes from the end of a personal **blog** written by a learner.

In pairs, discuss:

- the purpose of the text
- the intended audience
- why the audience might choose to read this text
- the structure of the text – how it is organised and linked
- whether this structure is likely to appeal to the audience and why.

Home   Blog   Photos   About

TO DO – OR NOT TO DO . . .

Okay, so is there a right way to decide what to do? What's more important? My feelings or the feelings of others? I ask myself this every day. Here's what I know, friends:

- Don't do anything that harms other people.
- Don't forget that your own wishes are important.
- Remember to listen to your emotions – let them guide you.

Easy? Maybe!

4 Write a paragraph explaining the purpose of the choices of simple and **minor sentences** in the blog, and the effect they have on the reader.

5 The two extracts in this session are aimed at similar audiences, but they were written in different contexts. 'The importance of conscience' is a detailed text by a professional writer and published by a well-respected and successful publisher. Before being published, it would have been legally checked and professionally edited. 'To do – or not to do . . .' is a short, personal, self-published online blog with a much smaller number of readers.

In pairs, discuss:

- the differences in language and punctuation choices and how they contribute to the overall effect
- the attitudes of the writers towards the topic in both texts
- how readers might respond to and value the content of both texts.

- How confident do you feel about understanding the influence of context on texts?
- How could this skill help you in later life?

Key words

minor sentence: a sentence that does not contain a main verb

Reading tip

When assessing the value and content of a text, think about who has written it, why and where it is published. Remember that a text's popularity doesn't always mean that the information is useful or necessarily accurate.

Summary checklist

☐ I can use reading strategies to identify key information in a non-fiction text and discuss its implications.

☐ I understand how the placement of different sentence types supports the purpose of a text.

☐ I can analyse language and purpose in related texts, and explain how context affects reader reaction.

> 2.2 Join the police

In this session, you will:

- identify the purpose, audience and structural features of a text
- explore the views of others on a complex topic
- use colons and semi-colons for effect.

Getting started

In pairs, discuss occasions when authority figures have helped and guided you. They might be teachers, police officers and other adults. What do you think are the challenges and rewards of being an authority figure?

A rewarding career

Read the following informative text, which comes from a UK police website.

| Home | Your Local Police | Join the Force | Latest News | Safety Guidelines | Contact Us |

Why should you become a police officer?

Joining the police will change your life; it will also change the lives of the community you serve. When you become a police officer, you are given power: the power to help people.

You will help people by protecting them. You will help people by reassuring them. You will help communities to be safe. You will help communities by preventing and solving crime.

When you join us, you will learn new skills; skills that will stay with you for life.

Is it the career for me?

Becoming a police officer is one of the best careers you can choose, but it isn't for everyone. Keeping people safe is a physical, mental and emotional challenge, but we will help you learn how to:

- handle difficult situations in a calm, confident manner
- develop excellent people skills and help all members of the public

- solve problems in a **decisive** way and take on new challenges

- work as a team and use your powers effectively

- investigate and solve crimes, and give evidence in court.

If that sounds appealing, we want to hear from you!

What are the rewards?

The main reward is **job satisfaction**. There is nothing more fulfilling than helping to protect the community, but you will also do a job where every day is different. Officers often say that no two days are the same, and the variety and unpredictable nature of policing is what keeps it interesting.

In practical terms, you will also receive a **competitive salary**, private healthcare and discounts from many shops and restaurants.

What training is offered?

Over three months, we will train you to the highest standards. You will learn in a classroom situation, but you will also spend time with trained officers, accompanying them and learning how to handle real-life situations. We will teach you how to:

- handle public safety and dangerous events

- use intelligence and investigative skills to solve crimes

- use technology to protect the public

- apply the law correctly.

If you want to make your community a safer and happier place, come and join the police.

---

decisive: being able to make decisions quickly
job satisfaction: the feeling of enjoyment that a person gets from their work
competitive salary: a rate of pay that compares well to other jobs

1   In pairs, discuss:

- what the purpose (or purposes) of the text might be

- who the intended audience is

- why the audience might choose to read the text

- the structure of the text – how it is organised and linked.

2   Use an appropriate reading strategy to find examples in the text that present being a police officer as a highly positive choice of career.

3   Use your notes from Activities 1 and 2 to discuss the implications of what you have read in pairs. Base your discussion on whether or not you agree with the three views below. Give reasons for your opinion.

Reading tip

When scanning (searching for key information), use the headings and subheadings of a text to break your scanning into manageable search areas.

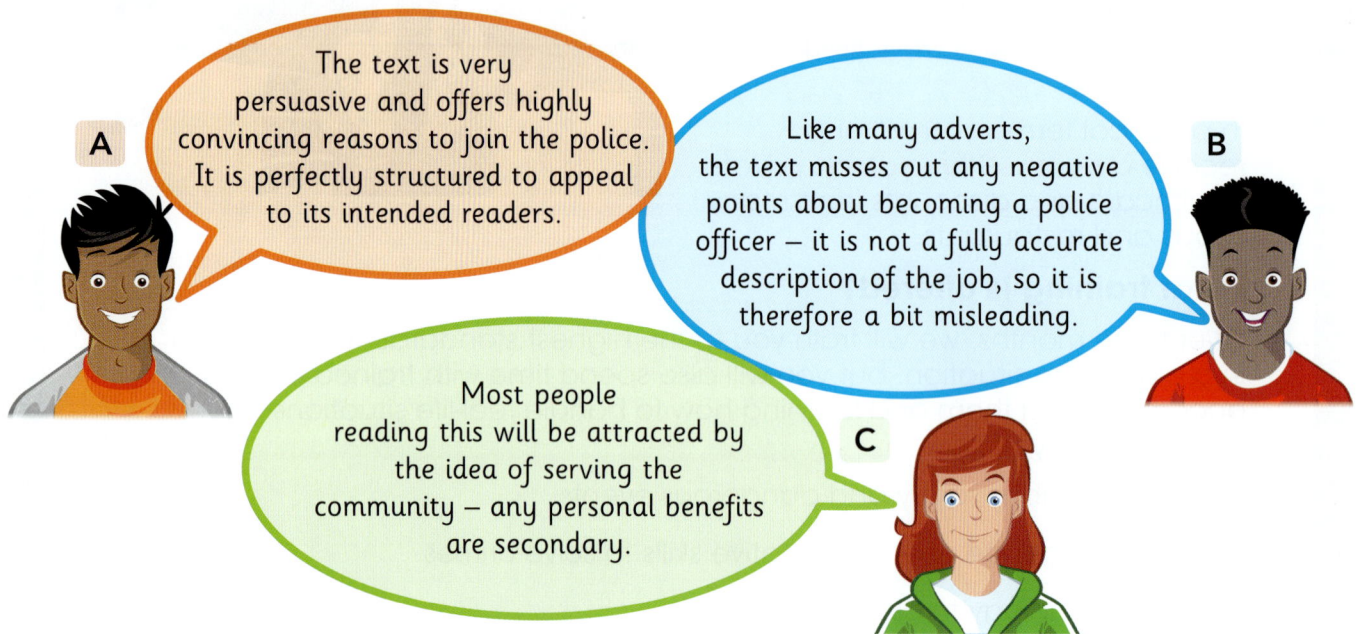

A
The text is very persuasive and offers highly convincing reasons to join the police. It is perfectly structured to appeal to its intended readers.

B
Like many adverts, the text misses out any negative points about becoming a police officer – it is not a fully accurate description of the job, so it is therefore a bit misleading.

C
Most people reading this will be attracted by the idea of serving the community – any personal benefits are secondary.

This is a complex topic, so choose language carefully to express ideas. Focus on keeping the discussion going and exploring points in detail. Make sure you allow each other opportunities to speak.

Peer assessment

Feed back to your partner on their speaking and listening skills. Comment on:

- whether they spent enough time exploring the given views in detail

- how clearly and confidently they discussed complex ideas.

Language focus

Colons and semi-colons are mainly used to help organise information in sentences. However, these punctuation marks can also be used for deliberate effect. For example, consider the difference between these two sentences:

- Police officers are very aware of one key thing about applying the law and that is fairness.
- Police officers are very aware of one key thing about applying the law: fairness.

Both sentences are correctly punctuated, but the colon in the second sentence strongly emphasises the word 'fairness' by making the reader pause before saying it.

Semi-colons can also suggest a relationship between ideas and give different shades of meaning. For example:

- Police officers are there to serve their community. Looking after people is the key part of their job.
- Police officers are there to serve their community; looking after people is the key part of their job.

The full stop in the middle of the first example gives the statement a factual tone. It invites the reader to stop, creating a 'distance' between the two ideas. In the second example, the semi-colon functions like the word 'because'. It brings the ideas closer together and emphasises the link between service, community and caring for others.

4   Choose one of the three views from Activity 3 and write a paragraph summarising your thoughts about it.

Use colons and semi-colons for organisation and effect. Use standard English to make your points in a formal, logical way.

Summary checklist

☐ I can identify and comment on the purpose, audience and structural features of a text.

☐ I can contribute to an effective discussion on different views of a complex topic.

☐ I can use colons and semi-colons to organise my writing and create different effects.

> 2.3 The art detective

In this session, you will:

- read aloud with confidence and expression
- discuss your own and others' views about an article
- summarise points of agreement and disagreement from a discussion
- write a descriptive account.

Getting started

Think about any detective stories you know. How is the job of detective presented in books and films? Would you like to be a detective in real life? Discuss your thoughts in pairs.

The art detective

Arthur Brand is an art detective. One of Brand's most famous cases involved finding a famous painting by Pablo Picasso, which had been missing for 20 years. In the following article by Joseph Bullmore, from *Gentleman's Journal*, Brand describes his experiences. He explains what happens when art is stolen.

1   Read the article aloud in pairs. Read alternate paragraphs, concentrating on reading ahead and pronouncing the words accurately. Use your voice to express the entertaining and exciting parts of the article.

Speaking tip

Varying the volume, pace and pitch of your voice can help bring a text to life. Use pauses to create drama, and speed up at moments of excitement. Spend time experimenting with different volumes to create different effects.

Confessions of an art detective

Within two years of a piece of art going missing, the police give up. And that's when I step in. My goal is to get the art back – and quickly, because I know there are **gangsters** driving around with priceless paintings in the boots of their cars, which isn't exactly the best place to keep them.

I start to ask around and I call all the people I know. Finally, when I'm certain that somebody has the piece I call them and listen to their reaction. Usually they say: 'What are you talking about?' and then they hang up. But in a couple of days, when they've had time to think about it, they'll call me back. And then the talks begin.

It's sometimes scary, but it's also great fun in these situations. Most of these people have a pretty good sense of humour.

The Picasso I found is considered to be one of his very best – he kept it in his own home. It was sold to an art dealer who sold it to a **sheikh** who put it on his boat, and it was stolen from there. Only a few people have ever set eyes on it.

I started to ask around, and after four years of work I found the current **possessor** – a businessman, who got it as a payment, and had no idea it had been stolen. He was very nervous. Eventually I managed to get it back. And for one night, I put it on my wall before handing it over.

An **auction house** then told me it could be worth more than $70m. But I don't make any money on these big cases. Nobody hired me, after all. But I don't do it for the money. I do it for the love of art. And the love of the job. I stopped watching action movies as soon as I became an art detective. Nothing is as exciting as real life.

> **gangsters:** criminals

> **sheikh:** an Arab leader
>
> **possessor:** owner
>
> **auction house:** a company that holds public sales where goods are sold to the highest bidder

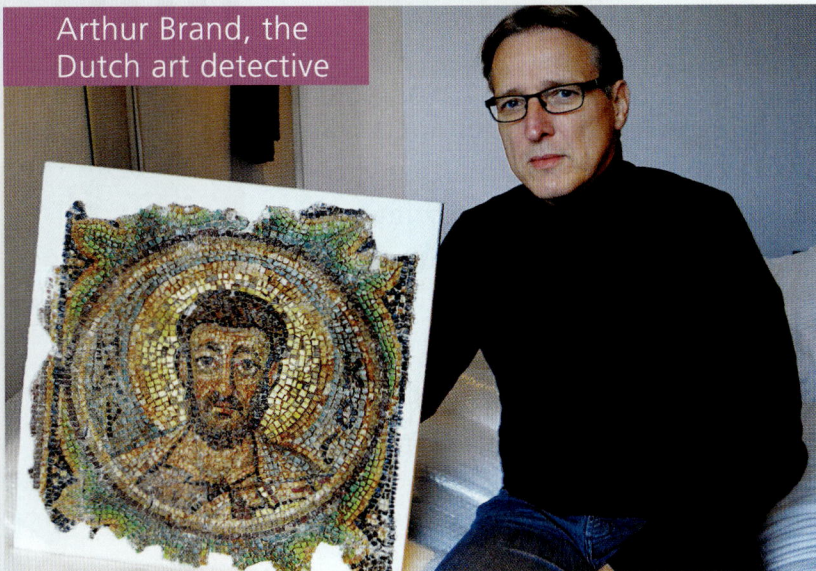

Arthur Brand, the Dutch art detective

2 The article reveals a lot about Arthur Brand's experiences.

In groups, discuss what this information suggests about him. Use the statements below to begin your discussion, exploring points of agreement and disagreement. Use information from the article to support your own views and challenge other people's. As you talk, make brief notes on the points made by group members.

Arthur Brand:

- is driven by a love for art

- enjoys the glamour of his job

- does a useful and helpful job

- seems to live a very privileged life

- is someone to admire

- has a job that many people would like to do

- is not a proper detective.

3 Using your notes from Activity 2, write a summary of the different views expressed within your group. Start by summarising the points you agreed on, then focus on areas of disagreement. Explain why you disagreed on these points.

- How useful are your notes from Activity 2 in recording people's views?

- What were the challenges of Activity 3?

4 Imagine you are Arthur Brand, sitting in a chair in your apartment late at night. On your wall is an extremely valuable print that you have spent years looking for and have finally found. The print uses shapes and colours to present an odd version of people's faces. You can see a copy of the print here.

Describe the print and your feelings as you look at it. Give some details about how you found it. Remember to think carefully about the character of Arthur Brand to convey his voice convincingly. Take care with your spelling. Write 250 words.

Listening tip

Making notes as you listen to other people can be challenging. Before you begin, make a table showing people's names with a space to record their views. Keep your notes brief, using key words to summarise views.

You could start like this:

There it was. After all this time, it hung on my wall. I relaxed in my leather chair and looked at its striking red and black imagery and the strange faces. Their eyes seemed to float as they looked at me: they were both alarming and amazing.

Summary checklist

☐ I can read a non-fiction text aloud with confidence and expression.

☐ I can contribute effectively to a group discussion, exploring my own and other people's views.

☐ I can summarise points from a discussion and explain areas of disagreement.

☐ I can write an imaginative descriptive account in a particular voice.

Writing tip

Descriptive writing relies partly on sensory descriptions – often what you can see. But it is also about the feeling and atmosphere you are trying to create, so make sure you think about the emotions you are trying to convey as you plan your writing.

❯ 2.4 Young detectives

In this session, you will:

- give a dramatic performance of a scene from a detective story
- explore the characters, events and tone of a detective story
- consider the effect of story structure.

Getting started

Here is a list of some elements of the story you will read in this session. In pairs, guess what will happen in the story, how it will end and what the various characters might do in the story.

- a valuable painting
- a large building called Old Park House
- Dan Robinson, a student

Continued

- Dan's three friends – Jeff, Liz and Mickey
- Sir Jasper Ryde, owner of Old Park House
- a group of tourists
- a large, unnamed man
- a small, unnamed and nervous man.

The Case of the Missing Masterpiece

You are going to read an extract from *The Case of the Missing Masterpiece* by Terrance Dicks. It is a fictional story about a group of young detectives who try to solve the mystery of a valuable painting (a masterpiece) that has been stolen from a museum called Old Park House.

The main character is Dan Robinson. He and his friends, Jeff, Liz and Mickey, visit Old Park House, hoping to find some clues. Dan plans to use the same methods that the famous fictional detective Sherlock Holmes uses to find out what happened.

The extract starts with the four friends looking at the blank wall where the painting used to hang. They then perform a reconstruction of the crime – a common police investigation technique used in real life. In a reconstruction, the crime is acted out to help people remember key events and details.

Extract 1

'Well, there it is,' said Liz. 'Or rather there it isn't!'

Jeff nodded. 'Well, don't just stand there, Sherlock. Detect something!'

Dan knew they were only teasing, but his heart sank all the same.

Here there was nothing. Just a light patch of **unfaded** wall where the picture had once hung. Even Sherlock Holmes wouldn't have been able to make anything of that.

Or would he?

An **oak-panelled** door had opened and a man stood looking at them. He was tall, and thin, he wore a baggy brown suit,

unfaded: fresh, not showing signs of fading

oak-panelled: made up of flat wooden pieces

and there was a plaster across his **balding** forehead. This was Sir Jasper Ryde – owner of Old Park House and ex-owner of the stolen painting.

They all gave embarrassed grins. All except Dan. His heart was pounding, but he forced himself to speak up. 'I know this sounds daft but we were thinking about investigating this crime.'

Sir Jasper stared at him in astonishment, and Dan struggled on. 'I expect you're sick of the whole business by now. But if you could spare a minute or two to talk about it . . . '

Sir Jasper was delighted. 'I shall be happy to assist your investigations in any way I can. Shall we go into my study?'

Dan found he couldn't think of anything sensible to ask.

A sudden inspiration came to his rescue. 'Since we're right here on the spot, why don't we reconstruct the crime instead of just talking about it?'

Sir Jasper jumped up enthusiastically, and immediately took charge. 'You all go outside and pretend to be stealing the painting. I'll be sitting here reading, just as I was on the actual night.'

He bustled them out into the gallery, where by now a few tourists were wandering about.

'What do we do now?' whispered Jeff.

'You heard him,' said Dan cheerfully. 'Steal the painting. You and Mickey can be the **robbers**.'

Jeff made vague cutting motions, and Mickey jumped up and down making great slashing sweeps that would have had the painting in shreds. The door to the study was **flung** open, and Sir Jasper appeared shouting, 'Aha, caught in the act!'

Dan thought it was time to intervene. 'Did you actually say that?'

'Well, no,' confessed Sir Jasper. 'I think I probably said something brilliant like "Er . . ."'

'And what did you see?'

'The small one was at the painting, and the big one was holding a torch. The one cutting seemed to be working very carefully.'

balding: having lost some hair due to age

robbers: thieves
flung: moved or pushed forcefully

1   Most of this scene is written as dialogue, which shows the different characters' personalities, as well as adding some humour.

Perform this extract in groups of three. Choose one each of the three speaking roles – Dan, Jeff and Sir Jasper. Begin your performance from the second line of the story.

Start by identifying the lines you will speak. Learn them if you can, or write them out as notes for when you perform. Think how you can use your voice and movement to bring out the ideas and personalities in the scene.

Here are some prompts for each character:

Dan: You feel under pressure because you have told your friends you could solve the case, but now you are not sure. You are a little afraid when Sir Jasper arrives, but soon become confident and enjoy yourself as the scene develops.

Jeff: You have come along with Dan. You like him, but doubt he can solve the crime. You like to make jokes, but become a little embarrassed as the scene develops.

Sir Jasper: You are polite and a little shy, but very pleased and excited to help Dan and his friends. You become more animated as the scene develops.

> **Speaking tip**
>
> When acting out a scene, remember to use gesture and action to suggest character. Plan how you will move in each part of the scene, using the words to help you decide how the character feels.

Self-assessment

Assess your performance as a group:

- How effective was your planning and performance of the scene?
- Did your use of movement and voice convey the personality of the character?

2   Most detective stories rely on mystery to entertain the reader, but this story also uses humour. In pairs, discuss and make notes on:

- which events and characters seem comic and which seem serious
- how and why the characters and story might appeal to its audience.

3   Detective stories often follow a similar structure. For example, near the beginning of the story, there may be a chapter where the detective visits the scene of the crime and talks to witnesses.

Write a paragraph analysing the sequence of events in Extract 1 and the effect this creates. Write about:

- how Dan's character develops during the scene
- what the introduction of Sir Jasper adds to the story.

4   Detection is often about making deductions – working things out from clues. At the end of the extract, the actions of the thieves are briefly described.

Write a paragraph explaining:

- the thieves' actions and what they suggest about the kind of people they are
- how this information affects what you have already read – does it make the story less humorous, for example?

Summary checklist

☐ I can give a dramatic performance of a scene from a detective story, using voice, gesture and movement to express character.

☐ I can comment on characters and events in a story and identify its tone.

☐ I can analyse the effect of structural choices in a detective story.

> 2.5 Making deductions

In this session, you will:

- explore the implications of information in a story
- consider the process of deduction as a structural feature
- write a character study
- compare characters and ideas in two texts.

Getting started

In pairs, discuss how detectives are normally presented in stories. What personal qualities and skills do they usually have?

Now read another extract from *The Case of the Missing Masterpiece*. Sir Jasper has explained to Dan that the thieves took him through to his library.

Extract 2

Dan leaned over Sir Jasper, 'Imagine it's all happening again. Try to see the men again. How were they dressed?'

'Dark clothes,' said Sir Jasper, struggling to remember. 'They wore masks. Oh yes and the one who helped me was worried about his hat. He was wearing one of those woollen caps sailors sometimes wear. He kept **fiddling** with it, pulling it down to meet his mask.'

'Anything else? His voice? His hands?'

'The voice was just ordinary. There was something about his hands though . . . His hands were very white . . . and there was something else . . . a smell . . .'

Suddenly Dan **shoved** Mickey out of the way. 'Jeff, let him smell your hands.'

Puzzled, Jeff obeyed, and Sir Jasper said, 'Yes, that's it. That's it exactly.'

Jeff drew his hands back guiltily, and Dan stood up.
'I think that's all for now. Can I come back if I think of anything else?'

'Yes, of course.' Sir Jasper seemed almost disappointed that the demonstration was ended. 'It would be marvellous if you could find it,' he said. 'I was relying on selling it to save the old place.'

'Save it?' asked Liz. 'Save it from what?'

'Being sold. Torn down for flats and offices.'

Liz was horrified 'You wouldn't let them do that, surely?'

Old Park House had been part of their lives for as long as they could remember, and they suddenly realized how much they would miss it.

They were all in a much more serious mood. Solving the mystery had been a kind of exciting game up till now – the realization that Old Park itself was in danger had made it all much more important – and more worthwhile.

fiddling: adjusting or moving something around
shoved: pushed

Jeff looked at Dan. 'All right, mastermind, this is where you amaze us with a stream of brilliant deductions I suppose?'

'All right,' said Dan. 'The crime was carried out by two men. One is a professional criminal with several convictions for robbery, the other has no previous convictions, a fairly junior job in the antiques business, and a very nervous **disposition**.' Dan looked round at their astonished faces. 'Oh yes, and one more thing. The smaller of the criminals had bright red hair.'

> **disposition:** a person's manner and personality

1   At the end of the extract, Dan makes some deductions about the thieves. Later we find out that the smell on Jeff's hands was from a type of cleaning product that is often used to clean antiques. This helps Dan work out that one of the thieves has *a fairly junior job in the antiques business*.

In pairs, look back through both extracts and work out how Dan made his other deductions. Remember to organise your discussion so you take turns to suggest ideas.

2   Fictional detectives often have special intelligence and abilities. Why do you think that writers portray their main characters in this way? Write a paragraph explaining:

•   what skills Dan has and what impression this creates of him

•   what it suggests about the process of solving crimes.

3   Deductions are a key part of the structure of detective stories (e.g. Dan's deductions here are the first step towards solving the mystery). Moments like this are also used for deliberate effect, such as changing the way the reader sees a central character.

Here is what one learner has said about this effect.

> Rather than seeing the story through Dan's eyes, it places the reader in the position of Dan's friends – amazed at his skills, rather than being like him. It makes Dan seem like a hero.

Do you agree? Why or why not? Use quotations from the extract to support your ideas.

4   Compare how the fictional Dan Robinson and the real-life Arthur Brand (the art detective you read about in Session 2.3) are presented. Make notes on:

- why each detective wants to solve the mystery – what motivates them

- what this suggests about the values of the detectives.

5   Write an account of the character of Dan Robinson. Give a summary of Dan's actions and motivations based on both extracts from the story. Explain why Dan is likely to appeal to the novel's intended audience.

Write 200 words. Use any strategies you know to ensure your spelling is accurate, and take care with your handwriting.

Summary checklist

- ☐ I can analyse the meaning and implications of information in a story.
- ☐ I understand the effect of structural choices such as the steps of deduction in detective fiction.
- ☐ I can write a character study, exploring actions and motivation.
- ☐ I can interpret and compare characters and ideas in two texts.

> 2.6 Detective fiction

In this session, you will:

- identify the conventions of detective fiction
- consider the purpose of a text and whether it is biased
- explore a writer's language and grammar choices
- listen to and summarise opinions on detective fiction, and express your own.

Getting started

Why do people enjoy detective fiction and TV shows that feature police and detectives as the main characters?
In pairs, discuss the appeal of the genre.

Selling detective fiction

The following text appears on the homepage of an online bookstore that specialises in detective fiction. It has been written by the owner of the bookstore.

Home	Blog	Photos	About		Search

THE THRILL OF THE DARK

Detective fiction is the most satisfying genre of them all – it's also the most popular! After all, nothing beats reading about dark **deeds** and shadowy mysteries from the safety of our sofa. But what else is it about detective fiction that appeals to us?

Well, I think it's because we like to challenge ourselves with seemingly impossible puzzles. We enjoy following super-smart detectives as they shine a torch into the shadows and bring light to the darkness. And, of course, we love to see the good guys beat the villains in the end! At the conclusion of a detective tale, a mystery is solved. It's very satisfying for the reader. These type of endings are very neat, with loose ends tied up and the feeling that the world is a safe and fair place after all.

deeds: actions

So in many ways, the genre is satisfyingly predictable. As well as a detective with a great mind and slightly odd personality, there's often an assistant who, like us, is puzzled by the detective's methods.

We also expect to meet villains driven by greed and explore some memorable settings, such as tough cities or old houses. There are clues for the detective (and us) to solve, as well as clues that turn out to be misleading but are all part of the fun.

Customers say they like the familiarity of detective fiction, but they also like those stories that end unexpectedly or that feature unusual characters. What type of detective stories do you like? Check out some of the new titles we have in store – there's plenty to choose from!

1 Read the text.

   a Make notes on the **conventions** of detective fiction that are mentioned in the text.

   b List any of these conventions that you can find in the extracts from *The Case of the Missing Masterpiece* from Sessions 2.4 and 2.5.

2 In pairs, discuss the purpose of this text. Consider:

   • who has written it, why they might have written it, and where it is published

   • whether the text shows **bias**.

> ### Key words
>
> **conventions:** the 'rules' of how a story is told or a piece of writing is set out
>
> **bias:** prejudice for or against a particular person, group or idea

> ### Reading tip
>
> Remember that there is a difference between an opinion based on a range of evidence and a biased opinion. Biased writing gives opinions based on personal viewpoints and some facts, but it deliberately ignores any facts that contradict the view it takes.

3 The writer uses an extended metaphor based on ideas of dark and light in the title and the first two paragraphs of the text. Analyse what this metaphor suggests about:

   • the themes of detective stories

   • the morals of the detectives and the villains that they *beat . . . in the end.*

4   Most of the time, the writer addresses the reader using the plural
     pronouns 'we' and 'us'. This suggests that readers share his opinions
     about detective fiction.

     Write a brief analysis of the effect of this grammatical choice in the
     text. Why might the writer want to imply a link with the reader, and
     how is that related to the purpose of the text?

5   You are going to listen to some readers talking about detective
     fiction. As you listen, make notes on each reader's preferences
     and experiences of the genre. Then write a summary of these
     different views, explaining how each reader's experiences affect
     their opinions.

6   As a class, describe some detective stories you have read and
     enjoyed. Make some recommendations to each other – which
     stories do you think other learners would enjoy?

Key word
pronoun: a word that stands in for a noun to avoid repetition ('I', 'you', 'him', 'hers', 'its', etc.)

Listening tip
Use a system to keep notes when listening to people's views. You could use a table to summarise multiple views, but make sure that you clearly label speakers' names and copy down brief key phrases accurately.

Summary checklist

- [ ] I can recognise and comment on the conventions of detective fiction.
- [ ] I can analyse the purpose of a text and assess whether it shows bias.
- [ ] I can analyse the meaning and effect of a writer's language and grammar choices.
- [ ] I can understand and summarise a variety of attitudes towards detective fiction.

Check your progress

Answer the following questions.

1. Explain how the context in which an article is written and published can influence a reader's reaction to it.

2. Using examples, explain how colons and semi-colons can create different effects.

3. Give some tips about reading aloud. How can you use your voice to make a text interesting to listen to?

4. Explain different ways you can use movement and gesture in a drama scene to convey character and action.

5. Explain how detectives are shown in crime fiction. What qualities do they have?

6. Summarise the conventions of crime fiction.

Project

In detective stories, the main character can be a private investigator, someone working for the police or even a normal person.

In groups, you will research detective figures in fiction from around the world. You will explore how detectives are presented and what features they have in common.

As a group, make a list of detective figures in stories you have read. Then do some research into stories from a range of times and cultures. You could find out about detectives in adult fiction such as Auguste Dupin (the first detective character in literature), Bhaduri Moshai, Philip Marlowe, Mme Ramotswe or Miss Marple. Remember to look at detectives in children's literature too, such as the Diamond Brothers or Young Sherlock Holmes. Try to read some extracts from books that these characters feature in.

Next, explore the qualities and styles of these detectives. You could consider:

- gender – are there typical characteristics of female and male detectives?
- details of their personal lives – are they generally happy, satisfied people?
- attitudes to authority – do they follow rules or do they challenge authority?
- their motivations for fighting crime.

As you work in your group, allocate roles for your research. For example, one of you might focus on children's literature, or one of you may have detailed knowledge of the genre already and could be the 'expert adviser'.

Once you have discussed your findings as a group, prepare a five-minute presentation for the class.

Decide what level of visual support you might need. For example, you could show some illustrations from the texts. Explain what you have discovered and read brief passages from the texts.

3 'The Red-Headed League'

In this unit, you will read a detective story called 'The Red-Headed League' by Sir Arthur Conan Doyle. It was written in 1891 and features the famous fictional detective Sherlock Holmes. You will explore the structure of the story, the characters and ideas about morality.

> 3.1 The red-headed visitor

In this session, you will:

- work out the meaning of unfamiliar words
- read and interpret information in the opening of a mystery story
- consider the impact of structural events
- explore the presentation of characters in two texts.

Getting started

In pairs, look at and discuss the pictures on this page. What do they suggest about Sherlock Holmes? What else do you know about the character and the stories he features in?

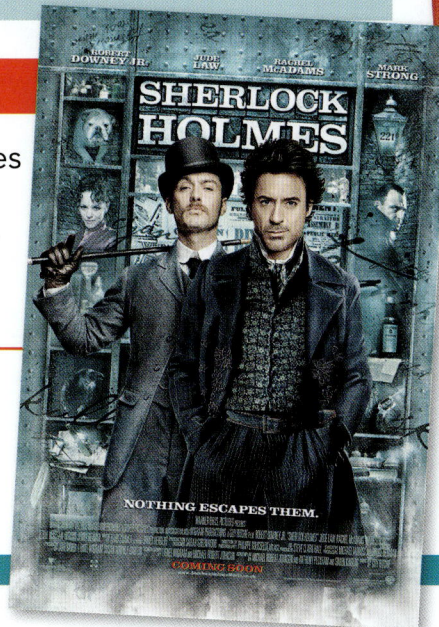

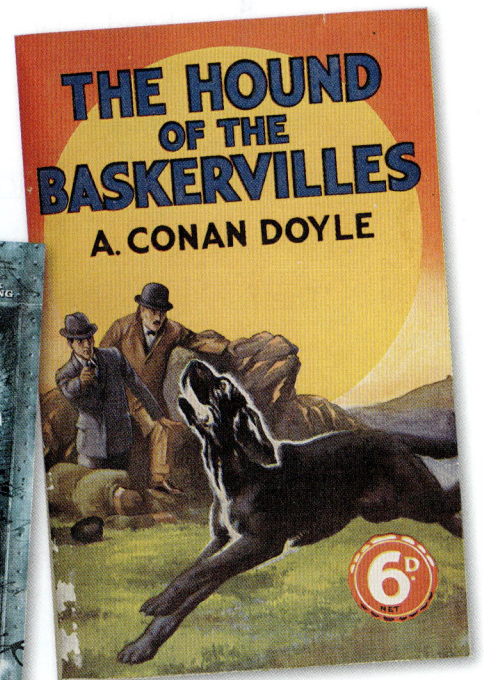

'The Red-Headed League'

Read the first extract. The story is told by Dr John Watson, who assists Sherlock Holmes with his investigations. As the story begins, a red-haired man called Jabez Wilson has arrived at Holmes's apartment to ask for help. Wilson feels he is the victim of a mysterious joke. He has brought a newspaper to show Holmes – it has a strange advertisement in it. The extract starts with Holmes making some impressive deductions about Wilson.

Extract 1

I had called upon my friend, Mr Sherlock Holmes, and found him in conversation with a very **stout**, **florid-faced**, elderly gentleman with fiery red hair. There was nothing remarkable about the man save his <u>blazing</u> red head.

Sherlock Holmes shook his head with a smile. '<u>Beyond</u> the obvious facts that he has done **manual labour**, that he has been in China, and that he has done a <u>considerable</u> amount of writing lately, I can <u>deduce</u> nothing else.'

Mr Jabez Wilson started up in his chair. 'How did you know that I did manual labour?'

'Your right hand is larger than your left and the muscles are more developed.'

'But the writing?'

'What else can be <u>indicated</u> by that right **cuff** so very shiny?'

'Well, but China?'

'The fish that you have tattooed above your right wrist is quite **peculiar** to China.'

Mr Jabez Wilson laughed heavily.

'Can you not find the advertisement, Mr Wilson?'

'Yes, I have got it now,' he answered with his thick finger planted halfway down the column. 'Here it is. This is what began it all. You just read it for yourself, sir.'

stout: heavily built
florid-faced: red-faced
manual labour: working with your hands

cuff: the end part of a sleeve
peculiar: special or specific

'TO THE RED-HEADED LEAGUE: there is now another **vacancy** open which <u>entitles</u> a member of the League to a salary of £4 a week for purely <u>nominal</u> services. All red-headed men are <u>eligible</u>. Apply to Duncan Ross, Fleet Street.'

> **vacancy:** an available job

Holmes <u>chuckled</u>. 'Mr Wilson, tell us all about yourself.'

'I have a small business at Coburg Square. I used to be able to keep two assistants, but now I only keep one; and I would have a job to pay him but that he is willing to come for half wages.'

'What is the name of this youth?' asked Sherlock Holmes.

Language focus

In older texts, you may come across unfamiliar words. There are several ways in which you can try and work out their meaning.

Context is a good starting point – read the words around the unfamiliar word in the sentence and also think about what is happening in the story at that point. For example, consider the sentence, *There was nothing remarkable about the man save his blazing red head.* You know that the speaker is making a comment on someone's appearance, so you can make a sensible guess that 'remarkable' means 'distinctive' or 'noticeable'.

You can also use your knowledge of **morphology**. In the case of 'remarkable', you can see that the pattern of the word suggests that is made up of three parts – the **prefix** 're-', the **root word** 'mark' and the **suffix** '-able'. Using word patterns and **etymology**, you may work out that 're-' means 'again', 'marquer' is French for 'note', and '-able' means 'capable of'.

Finally, thinking about similar words can help you work out the meaning of a word you don't know. For example, you might be familiar with the words 'remark', 'marked' or 'marking', which will give you a clue that 'remarkable' is connected to ideas of 'comment on' and 'noticeable'.

Key words

morphology: the study of how words are formed and their relationship with other words

prefix: letters added to the beginning of a word to make a new word with a different meaning

root word: the basic form of a word that other words with related meanings are based on

suffix: letters added to the end of a word to make a new word with a different meaning

etymology: the origins of a word

1   In pairs, work out the meanings of the underlined words in the extract using appropriate strategies. Create a **glossary** of their definitions.

Reading tip

It can sometimes be helpful to use a combination of techniques to work out the meaning of unfamiliar words. Your main strategy is likely to be the context of the sentence, but it is good practice to research the etymology of new words too. You can do this by using a dictionary or an online search engine.

Key word

glossary: an alphabetical list of words or phrases from a text, with their meanings

- Which strategies did you find most useful when completing Activity 1?
- Which words did you find most difficult to define? Why do you think that was?

2   Reread the extract and make notes on:
   - how Holmes works out the details about Wilson's life and experiences
   - what this implies about Holmes's character and skills.

3   There are three important structural events at the start of this story: the introduction of the detective; the introduction of a possible victim; and the establishment of a mysterious plot element.

Answer the following questions. Try to be precise and perceptive in your responses.

   a   *A very stout, florid-faced, elderly gentleman with fiery red hair.* What does the language in this description suggest about Jabez Wilson?

   b   How does the introduction of the advertisement create a sense of mystery – what questions does it raise for the reader?

4   In Sessions 2.4 and 2.5, you studied *The Case of the Missing Masterpiece*, which also featured a victim figure.

   a   Using an appropriate strategy, locate details about the victims in both stories. Make brief notes about the way they react to their experiences.

b   Victims are usually presented as **sympathetic characters**. Using well-chosen details from both texts, explain how you react to Jabez Wilson and Sir Jasper Ryde.

Summary checklist

- [ ] I can use a variety of strategies to work out the meaning of unfamiliar words in an older text.
- [ ] I can work out the implied meaning of information in the opening of a detective story.
- [ ] I can comment on the impact of language and structure in a story.
- [ ] I can analyse how two victim figures are presented in different texts.

> 3.2 The assistant

In this session, you will:

- explore the implications of information in a mystery story
- consider the structural effects of introducing a new character
- improvise a conversation in character
- explore developing feelings of sympathy towards a character.

Getting started

In pairs, make some predictions about Jabez Wilson's involvement with the Red-Headed League. What do you think has happened? Why might he be seeking the help of a detective like Sherlock Holmes?

Read the next part of the story on the following page. Here, Wilson explains to Holmes how his assistant, Vincent Spaulding, encouraged him to apply for the job with the League, and then accompanied him to the League's office.

Extract 2

'His name is Vincent Spaulding, and he's not a youth, either. I should not wish a smarter assistant, Mr Holmes; and I know he could earn twice what I am able to give him.'

'It is not a common experience among employers.'

'Oh, he has his faults, too,' said Mr Wilson. '**Snapping away with a camera** and then diving down into the cellar to develop his pictures. That is his main fault, but he's a good worker. He came with this paper in his hand, and he says:

'Why, here's another vacancy on the League of the Red-Headed Men. It's worth a fortune to any man who gets it.'

'Tell me all about it,' said I.

'Well,' said he, showing me the advertisement, 'the League was founded by an American millionaire who was himself red-headed; when he died, he left his enormous fortune to men whose hair is of that colour. From all I hear it is **splendid** pay and very little to do.'

'But,' said I, 'there would be millions of red-headed men who would apply.'

'I have heard it is no use applying if your hair is anything but real bright, blazing, fiery red.'

'Vincent Spaulding seemed to know so much about it, so I ordered him to come right away with me and we soon found ourselves in the office. There was nothing in the office but a couple of wooden chairs and a table, behind which sat a small man with a head that was even redder than mine. He gazed at my hair. Then suddenly he congratulated me.

'My name,' said he, 'is Mr Duncan Ross. When shall you be able to enter upon your new duties?'

'Well, it is a little awkward, for I have a business already,' said I.

'Oh, Mr Wilson!' said Vincent Spaulding. 'I should be able to look after that for you.'

'**What would be the hours?**' I asked.

snapping away with a camera: taking photographs

splendid: excellent

what would be the hours?: how long do I have to work?

'Ten to two.'

'And the pay?'

'£4 a week.'

'And the work?'

'Well, you have to be in the office, or at least in the building, the whole time to copy out the Encyclopedia.'

1   Readers of mystery stories behave almost like detectives, trying to assess the actions and behaviour of the characters.

Look at the information given about Vincent Spaulding and in pairs, discuss:

   • aspects of his behaviour that seem strange

   • aspects of his behaviour that seem helpful

   • whether you think Spaulding will emerge as a villainous character or an innocent one by the end of the story.

2   Writers plan carefully when to introduce a character and the information they will give the reader.

Write a paragraph explaining the effect of introducing Spaulding at this point in the story: how does it help increase the feeling of mystery?

3   There are several suspicious things about the job Wilson has been offered:

   • The rate of pay is excellent for an easy job with short hours (£4 a week was a lot of money at the time the story was written).

   • Copying out an encyclopedia seems a pointless task.

   • The job is only open to men with fiery red hair.

   • Ross offers Wilson the job immediately.

   • Spaulding seems very keen for Wilson to take the job.

In pairs, **improvise** a conversation between Jabez Wilson and Vincent Spaulding, in which they discuss the job with the League.

Key word
improvise: to perform without preparation

Imagine that Wilson has doubts about the job and Spaulding tries to persuade him to do it.

In your conversation, try to draw out ideas about the men's attitudes towards money. Start your conversation with Wilson saying: 'I'm not sure about this job, Vincent.'

4 Now listen to an audio recording of an imagined conversation between Wilson and Spaulding like the one you improvised for Activity 3. Make notes to answer the following questions.

    a How does Spaulding try to persuade Wilson to do the job?

    b What is the main reason Wilson decides to do the job and what does this imply about him?

    c Does listening to this conversation make you feel sympathy for Wilson or not? Why?

    d Describe the tone of voice used by the person reading Spaulding's part: what does it suggest about his personality?

Listening tip

When listening to texts being read aloud, think carefully about the tone used for characters' voices. The way an actor uses their voice can help you understand a bit more about the character's personality and attitudes. For example, an enthusiastic tone might indicate that the character is trying to be persuasive.

Summary checklist

☐ I can identify and understand the meaning and implications of information in a mystery story.

☐ I can explain the structural effects of introducing a new character at a particular point in a story.

☐ I can confidently improvise a conversation to express a character's feelings.

☐ I can listen to a dialogue between two characters and comment on how it develops feelings of sympathy.

> 3.3 The end of the League

In this session, you will:

- work out the meanings of unfamiliar words
- interpret details about a central character in a story
- identify and analyse information in a story
- write a formal report.

Getting started

If you were Holmes, what questions would you ask Wilson?
Make a list in pairs, then decide on the three most useful ones.

Read the next part of the story. Wilson starts by describing his first day working for the League.

Extract 3

'The table was set out ready for me, and Mr Duncan Ross was there to see that I got to work. He started me off upon the letter A, and then he left me. This went on day after day, Mr Holmes, and on Saturday the manager came in and **planked down** four golden **sovereigns** for my week's work. It was the same next week, and the same the week after. Every morning I was there at ten, and every afternoon I left at two.

'Eight weeks passed away like this, and then suddenly the whole business came to an end. I went to my work as usual, but the door was shut and locked, with a little square of cardboard on the middle of the panel. Here it is:

THE
RED-HEADED LEAGUE
IS DISSOLVED

planked down:
put down
sovereigns: coins

'I was <u>staggered</u>.'

'And what did you do then?' asked Holmes.

'I came right away to you.'

'And you did very <u>wisely</u>,' said Holmes. 'Your case is a remarkable one, and I shall be happy to look into it.'

'I want to find out about them, and who they are, and what their <u>object</u> was in playing this joke.'

'This assistant of yours – how long had he been with you?'

'About a month then.'

'Why did you pick him?'

'Because he was <u>handy</u> and would come cheap.'

'What is he like, this Vincent Spaulding?'

'Small, stout-built, very quick in his ways, no hair on his face, though he's **not short of thirty**.'

Holmes sat up in his chair in excitement. 'I thought as much,' said he. 'Have you ever observed that his ears are <u>pierced</u>?'

'Yes, sir.'

'That will do, Mr Wilson. I shall be happy to give you an opinion in a day or two.'

'Well, Watson,' said Holmes when our visitor had left us, 'what do you make of it all?'

'I make nothing of it,' I answered <u>frankly</u>. 'It is most mysterious.'

> **not short of thirty:** at least 30 years old

1   Use any appropriate strategies to work out the meaning of the underlined words. Write a glossary for them.

2   Readers will react in different ways to the character of Jabez Wilson. Look at these words that could be used to describe him:

    • greedy

    • a fool

    • pitiable

    • a victim.

    In small groups, discuss whether you agree or disagree with these descriptions of Wilson. Give reasons for your thinking, using references from the text.

3   By now, you will have realised that there is something suspicious about the Red-Headed League and that Vincent Spaulding is linked to the mystery in some way.

    On your own, make notes on:

    a   the apparent history and actions of the League

    b   key details about Vincent Spaulding and Duncan Ross

    c   any clues you have noted or suspicions you have.

    Decide how best to organise your notes – consider using a spider diagram or mind map, bullet points or a table.

4   In pairs, compare and discuss your lists from Activity 3. Work together to come up with some theories about what may have happened. Test your ideas by making specific references to the text. Sustain your discussion by exploring points of agreement and disagreement.

5   Imagine that you have been asked to write a report on the mystery so far. The purpose of the report is to clearly set out the background and events of Wilson's interaction with the League, any theories you have and to make suggestions about things that need to be investigated further.

Using your notes and discussions, plan and write your report. Remember to provide clear, logical and direct information. You should use the conventions of reports, including:

- sections with subheadings to organise the information

- organisational devices such as bullet points or numbered lists

- clear, direct language (avoid too many complex words)

- formal, standard English

- mostly simple and compound sentences.

Start by planning the structure of your report – make a list of the sections you will use.

Your completed report should be around 250 words. Focus on the accuracy of your spelling, using strategies to help you such as knowledge of morphology.

> **Writing tip**
>
> When writing reports, remember to make it clear to your reader when you are focusing on facts and when you are making suggestions based on theories or ideas. Reports are most effective when facts are presented first.

Peer assessment

In pairs, swap your reports and evaluate each other's writing.

- Has your partner presented the facts clearly?

- Have they made appropriate choices of language and sentence types?

- Are their structural choices effective? Is the report organised in a way that helps the reader?

Summary checklist

- ☐ I can choose appropriate strategies to work out the meaning of unfamiliar words.
- ☐ I can comment on interpretations of and reactions to a central character in a story.
- ☐ I can identify, analyse and discuss the implications of information in a story.
- ☐ I can plan and write a clear, well-structured report using appropriate features.

> 3.4 Investigating the street

In this session, you will:

- read an unseen text aloud
- discuss a series of clues and make predictions
- write and edit an ending to a mystery story involving tension, climax and release.

Getting started

Towards the middle of a story, a writer usually begins to prepare the reader for the ending by suggesting how it could conclude. In pairs, discuss stories where you used clues to predict the ending of a story. Did you enjoy this process? Why or why not?

In the next extract, Holmes and Watson visit the street where Jabez Wilson's business is situated. They meet Spaulding.

1 In groups of four, read the extract aloud. Focus on reading accurately and with confidence, varying your voice to bring out the drama.

Each person should read one of these parts:

- Watson's narration
- Holmes's dialogue
- Spaulding's dialogue
- Watson's dialogue.

Extract 4

Sherlock Holmes walked slowly up the street, looking at the houses. Finally, having thumped upon the pavement with his stick two or three times, he went up to the door and knocked. It was instantly opened by a bright-looking, clean-shaven young fellow, who asked him to step in.

'Thank you,' said Holmes, 'I only wished to ask you how you would go from here to **the Strand**.'

the Strand: a street in London

'Third right, fourth left,' answered the assistant promptly, closing the door.

'Smart fellow, that,' observed Holmes as we walked away. 'I have known something of him before.'

'**Evidently**,' said I, 'Mr Wilson's assistant counts for a good deal in this mystery. I am sure that you inquired your way in order that you might see him.'

'Not him.'

'What then?'

'The knees of his trousers.'

'And what did you see?'

'What I expected to see.'

'Why did you beat the pavement?'

'My dear doctor, this is a time for observation, not for talk.'

The road in which we found ourselves as we turned round the corner presented a contrast to the front. The footpaths were black with the hurrying pedestrians.

'Let me see,' said Holmes, standing at the corner, 'I should like just to remember the order of the houses here. There is Mortimer's, the newspaper shop, the City and Suburban Bank, the Vegetarian Restaurant, and McFarlane's **depot**. This business is serious . . . I shall want your help to-night.'

'At what time?'

'Ten will be early enough.'

'I shall be at Baker Street at ten.'

He waved his hand, turned on his heel, and disappeared in an instant among the crowd.

It was a quarter-past nine when I made my way to Baker Street and as I entered I heard the sound of voices. On entering his room, I found Holmes in conversation with two men, one of whom I recognised as Peter Jones, the official police agent, while the other was a long, thin, sad-faced man, with a very shiny hat.

'Watson, let me introduce you to Mr Merryweather, a bank director.'

evidently: clearly

depot: a large storage place

- How did reading your lines aloud help your confidence?
- How did you decide when to change the volume, pace and tone of your voice?

2   In this extract, Holmes begins to make some deductions about the mystery. Like Watson, the reader is not really sure what Holmes is looking for.

Make a list of what Holmes does. Use this list to make some guesses about what he is trying to discover.

3   In the extracts you will read in the next two sessions, the mystery is cleared up. In small groups, discuss the information given below and suggest different ways the story might end.

- Jabez Wilson had a pointless, well-paid job that took him away from his own business every day.

- Vincent Spaulding was very keen for Wilson to take the job.

- Spaulding was happy to look after Wilson's business and work for little pay.

- Spaulding spends a lot of time in the cellar and his trousers have dirty knees.

- Holmes has checked the pavement outside Wilson's business.

- Mr Merryweather's bank is behind Wilson's business.

4   Use the clues to write your own ending to the story. Set the scene inside the bank at night.

Remember that at the end of mystery stories, there is:

- a dramatic, tense scene

- a moment of climax as the hero confronts danger

- a feeling of release as the villain is caught and the danger ends.

Write the ending in the **first person** in the voice of Watson. Combine language techniques, sentence types and punctuation choices to help you create various effects such as tension and release.

Write 250 words. Make sure your handwriting remains fluent throughout.

Key words

first person: written from a single point of view, using pronouns such as 'I' and we'

Writing tip

When planning a story, it can sometimes help to work backwards – start by working out what happens in the final sentence and then decide what action comes before this.

Self-assessment

Reread your ending to evaluate it before redrafting it.

- How effective is your ending – does it create a sense of tension that is likely to engage your reader?
- How effective are your language choices – are there any better words you could use?

Summary checklist

☐ I can read an unseen text aloud confidently and accurately, using dramatic techniques for effect.

☐ I can explore layers of meaning in a story and use them to make predictions.

☐ I can plan, write and edit the ending of a story, combining various techniques for effect.

> 3.5 The dark cellar

In this session, you will:

- consider the effect of structural choices in a narrative
- explore how language choices contribute to the overall effect of a text
- practise writing descriptively, using aural and tactile images
- identify what makes an effective description.

Getting started

Mystery stories often contain interesting settings, such as old houses or dangerous parts of cities. In pairs, discuss your favourite settings from mystery stories. How do these settings add to the atmosphere of the story?

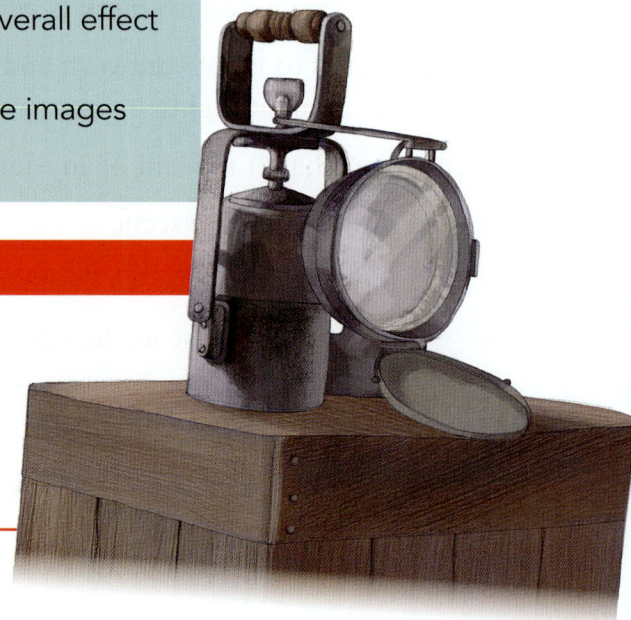

The next part of the story takes place in the cellar of the bank. Before it begins, Holmes reveals that he is expecting 'John Clay, thief and forger' to break in to the cellar.

Extract 5

Mr Merryweather stopped to light a **lantern**, and then **conducted** us down a dark passage, and into a huge cellar, which was piled with crates and massive boxes.

Holmes fell upon his knees upon the floor and, with the lantern and a **magnifying lens**, began to examine the cracks between the stones.

'Mr Merryweather will explain to you why the criminals of London take a considerable interest in this cellar.'

'It is our French gold,' whispered the director. 'The crate upon which I sit contains 2,000 **napoleons**.'

'I expect that within an hour matters will come to a head. In the meantime Mr Merryweather, we must put the screen over that lantern.'

'And sit in the dark?'

'These are daring men, and may do us harm unless we are careful. I shall stand behind this crate, and do you conceal yourselves behind those. Then, when I flash a light upon them, close in swiftly.'

Holmes left us in pitch darkness – such an absolute darkness as I have never before experienced. To me, there was something depressing in the sudden gloom, and in the cold dank air of the vault.

'They have **but one retreat**,' whispered Holmes. 'That is back through the house. I hope that you have done what I asked you, Jones?'

'I have two officers waiting at the front door.'

'Then now we must be silent and wait.'

What a time it seemed! My limbs were weary and stiff, for I feared to change my position; yet my nerves were worked up to the highest pitch of tension.

lantern: a portable lamp with a handle and shade
conducted: led
magnifying lens: a piece of glass for enlarging objects
napoleons: gold coins

but one retreat: only one way out of the cellar

1 Every story has a 'shape' – parts that add to the overall structure, shaping the **narrative** in a way that entertains the reader. For example, the structure of 'The Red-Headed League' so far could be broken down in the following way:

- the introduction of detective and victim figures

- the details and investigation of a mystery

- the introduction of a villain figure

- the introduction of a new, mysterious setting

- a gradual increase in tension.

In mystery stories, danger creates tension, and this leads to a climax in the story. In pairs, discuss and make notes on the way the writer creates tension in Extract 5. Explore the effect on the reader of the inclusion of:

- the night-time setting and the fact that the scene takes place underground

- the darkness and silence of the room

- the threat posed by John Clay

- the uncertain timing of Clay's arrival.

2 Now look more closely at the language the writer uses to create tension. Write a list of words and phrases that add to this overall effect. For example, you might look at the adjective-noun combination *absolute darkness*.

> **Key word**
>
> narrative: a series of connected events that are written or spoken

Reading tip

When exploring the effect of language, always think about its impact on the overall text, not just the sentence you are reading. As well as considering the meanings of individual words, think how they work alongside other words and structures to create and build the atmosphere.

Language focus

As well as visual images, aural and **tactile images** can help establish a distinctive atmosphere and help readers to imagine a scene. For example, when writing about scary situations, using aural imagery to refer to quiet, mysterious sounds can establish and build tension:

- Somewhere in the distance, I could hear the sound of a small animal moving slowly, its claws scraping across the stone floor.

The slow speed of the animal and uncertainty about what it is helps to create a fearful sensation.

Now read this example of tactile imagery:

- In the dark, I could feel the spider scuttle rapidly across my hand.

Here, the fear of spiders that many people naturally have is increased by the reference to movement and speed. Notice that in both examples, the lack of visual description of the animal and the spider heightens the sense of fear.

3 Imagine you are Watson sitting in the dark cellar. Write a 100-word description of your feelings, using the first-person voice throughout.

Use aural and tactile images, as well as other language devices, punctuation and sentence types, to create a sense of tension.

End your description with the arrival of John Clay.

4 Here is a learner's answer to the previous activity. In pairs, discuss why it is effective. What are the best parts of the response?

In the pitch darkness, my mind began to play tricks on me. I lost sense of the position of my companions in the cellar. Somewhere, I could hear Merryweather's thin breaths and Jones's heavy wheezing, but the sounds seemed to merge into one and swim around in the gloom. The regular torture of a steady drip of water leaking into the cellar was the only other sound to be heard. Regular as clockwork, it hit the cellar floor, as if it were counting down the minutes to certain doom. The cellar was damp and the moistness on my shirt collar was becoming uncomfortable. Suddenly, there was the sound of cracking beneath us.

Self-assessment

Reread your description from Activity 3.

- How does your answer compare to the learner's answer in Activity 4?
- What different language choices could you make to increase the sense of tension?

Evaluate and edit your own work before handing in a final draft.

Summary checklist

- ☐ I can analyse the effect of structural choices in a narrative.
- ☐ I can comment on how language choices contribute to the overall effect of a text.
- ☐ I can write descriptively, using effective choices of aural and tactile imagery and other techniques.
- ☐ I understand and can comment on what makes a description effective.

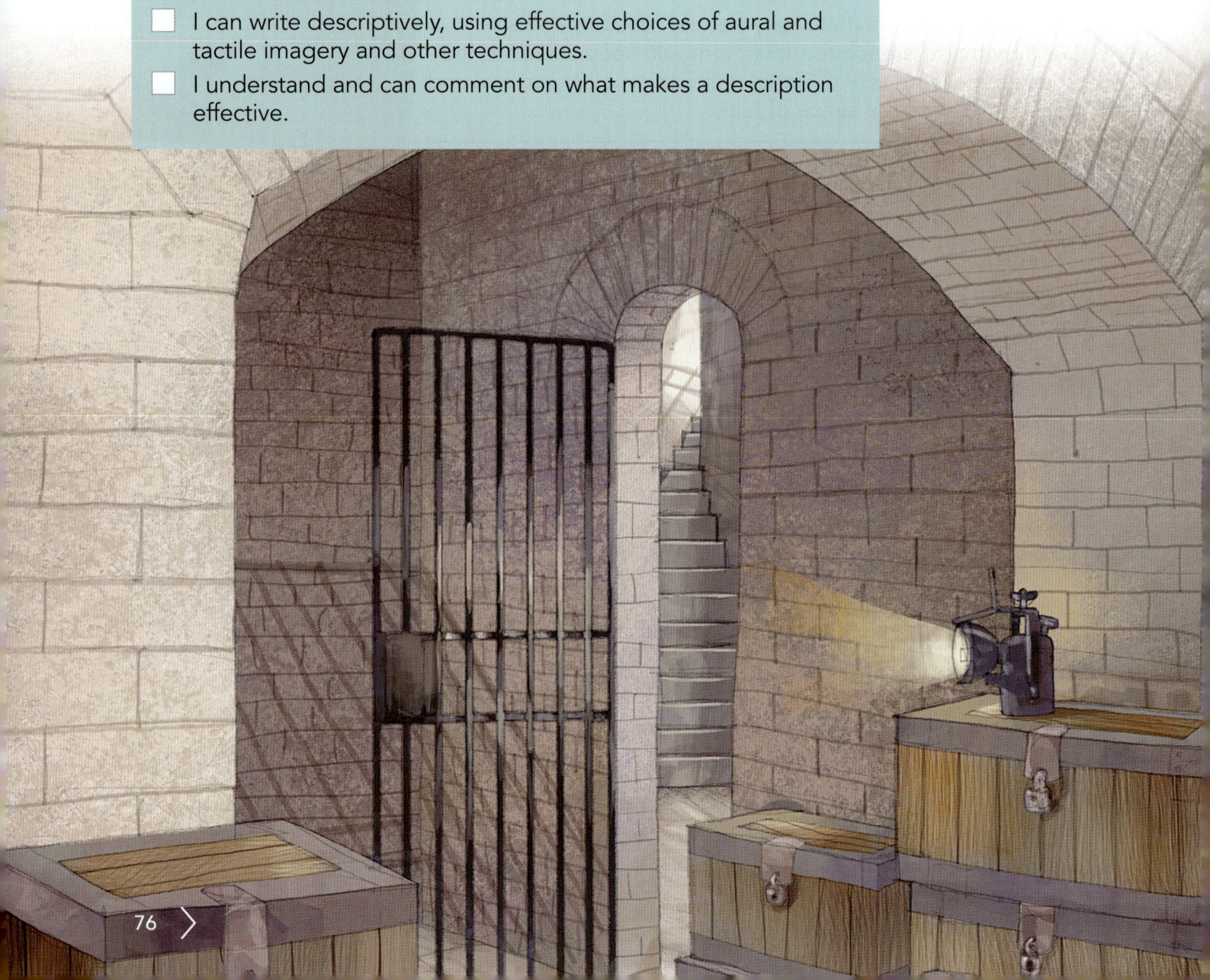

> 3.6 The solution

> **In this session, you will:**
>
> - express a personal response to the end of a mystery story
> - compare the way a theme is presented in two texts
> - explore how readers' reactions to stories are shaped by their experiences and beliefs.

> **Getting started**
>
> How do mystery stories usually end? Are they predictable or not? Do they have a twist in the tale? Think of some examples you have read and discuss them with a partner.

Read the final part of the story, where the mystery is solved and Holmes explains to Watson how he worked it out.

Extract 6

Suddenly my eyes caught the glint of a light.

At first it was a spark then it became a yellow line, and then a hand appeared.

With a tearing sound, one of the broad, white stones turned over and left a hole, through which peeped a boyish face. In another instant he stood at the side of the hole and was **hauling** after him a companion.

hauling: pulling

Sherlock Holmes had sprung out and seized the intruder. The other dived down the hole.

'It's no use, John Clay,' said Holmes. 'You have no chance at all.'

'So I see,' the other answered. 'I **fancy** that my pal is all right, though.'

fancy: imagine

'There are men waiting for him at the door,' said Holmes.

***

'You see, Watson,' he explained in the early hours of the morning, 'it was perfectly obvious that the only possible object of the advertisement of the League, and the copying of the Encyclopedia, must be to get Jabez Wilson out of the way for a number of hours every day. From the time that I heard of the assistant having come for half wages, it was obvious to me that he had some strong motive for securing the situation.'

'But how could you guess what the motive was?'

'I thought of the assistant vanishing into the cellar. He was doing something in the cellar – he was running a tunnel to some other building. I surprised you by beating upon the pavement with my stick. I was **ascertaining** whether the cellar stretched out in front or behind. Then I rang the bell, and, as I hoped, the assistant answered it. I hardly looked at his face. His knees were what I wished to see. You must yourself have remarked how stained they were. They spoke of those hours of **burrowing**. The only remaining point was what they were burrowing for. I walked round the corner, saw the City and Suburban Bank and felt that I had solved my problem.'

ascertaining: confirming, working out

burrowing: digging in the ground

1 This part of the story, where the mystery is explained, is called the **denouement**. In it, the reader discovers the solution to the mystery and what happens to the criminal.

You may have already guessed from the clues that John Clay and Vincent Spaulding are the same person. What effect does this extract have on you as a reader?

Write a brief explanation of your reaction to the solution to the mystery.

2 Mystery stories usually explore themes such as good and evil, power and human behaviour. By the end of a story, a reader understands the moral that the writer is expressing.

'The Red-Headed League' and *The Case of the Missing Masterpiece* (Sessions 2.4 and 2.5) both explore ideas about villains being caught. Here is what happens at the end of *The Case of the Missing Masterpiece*:

- Dan (the young detective) tracks down the two thieves to a hideout in the countryside

- the police arrest the thieves and they are sent to prison

- Dan and his friends are given a reward and appear in the newspapers

- the painting is returned to Sir Jasper

- Old Park House is saved and will not be knocked down.

Write a 200-word comparison of the endings of the two texts.

3 One important theme in Sherlock Holmes stories is the good moral values of the detective. In 'The Red-Headed League', Holmes and Watson act to stop John Clay taking money from the bank.

How does this connect to your own views about goodness in the real world? Discuss the view here, taking turns to explore the issues raised.

Key word

denouement: the final part of a story where things are explained

I think Holmes is a good and very moral character. He uses his skills to protect people and is motivated by trying to defeat evil. He is prepared to take risks and can be seen as a hero. He is a dedicated character who defends others. The ending reflects my views about moral values in the real world because I believe that humans should use their time and abilities to help others when they can.

4 'The Red-Headed League' was written in 1891 and contains references to ideas and objects from the past. To some modern readers, the story might seem old-fashioned, because the method of investigating the mystery seems basic compared to today's use of technology.

Read the following views of the story and discuss them in pairs. How do the experiences and opinions of each reader affect their view of the story?

Reading tip

Remember that although fiction is not real, it often reflects ideas and opinions about the real world. Always ask yourself what moral messages stories give out and whether you agree with them.

A
I love Sherlock Holmes stories and I've read most of them. The stories I like best are the ones where you don't know the solution until the last page.

B
I liked this story, but I prefer stories that keep you guessing about the identity of the villain. It's too obvious that Spaulding is the villain from the start.

C
This story is old-fashioned and predictable. It's always men who are the heroes and are shown doing exciting and noble things. I prefer stories with strong female characters.

5 Using the information from Activities 3 and 4 that you find helpful, write a paragraph explaining your own view of the story and those of others. Maintain a legible and fluent writing style.

Summary checklist

- [ ] I can clearly express a personal response to the ending of a mystery story.
- [ ] I can analyse and discuss themes and moral messages in more than one text.
- [ ] I can explain how readers' reactions to stories are shaped by their experiences and beliefs.

Check your progress

Answer the following questions.

1   Explain some of the different strategies that can be used to work out the meaning of unfamiliar words.

2   Using examples, explain the effect of introducing a suspicious character into a story and how it can contribute to the overall effect of a text.

3   What advice would you give about writing a report? Describe the tone and structure of this type of writing.

4   Explain how mystery stories usually end and give some tips for writing the end of a mystery tale.

5   Give an account of the typical narrative structure of a mystery story.

6   Explain, with examples, what the following statement means: 'Readers' experiences and beliefs affect how they respond to stories.'

Project

Having studied the ending of a short mystery story, you are now going to work in groups to explore the endings of other story genres.

With the help of your teacher, each group will choose a different type of short story to analyse. These might be stories from genres such as adventure, thriller, fantasy and science fiction. Once you have chosen your story, read it in your group and then focus on the ending of the story. You should explore:

*   the events at the end of the story
*   whether the story ends happily or badly for the main character(s)
*   whether all of the questions are resolved in the denouement
*   if it was an expected or unexpected ending – did you predict it?
*   your views about the ending – was it satisfying to read?
*   the moral ideas and themes that emerge.

Once you have discussed your thoughts, write a 300-word report summarising your findings. You can decide the best way to structure your report, but each group member should contribute to the writing.

Give a brief presentation to the class summarising the main findings of your report, deciding whether visual aids are appropriate. Finally, spend time reading the full reports of other groups.

Time

In this unit, you will explore how ideas about time are presented in a range of texts. You will study a selection of poems about the passing of time, read and discuss some non-fiction articles about the past and the future, and explore the genre of science fiction.

› 4.1 Moments in time

In this session, you will:

- read an unseen poem aloud
- explore a poet's themes and language choices
- write a poem in the style of a well-known poet
- give a personal response to a writer's work.

Getting started

In pairs, discuss the thoughts and emotions you have when the year comes to an end. Start by considering whether you feel sad, or if you are happy and looking forward to the new year. Try to explain your emotions clearly.

Poems by Su Tung P'o

You are going to read three poems by the 11th-century Chinese poet Su Tung P'o. They are all about specific moments in time.

1   Read the poem 'Autumn' aloud. Use the punctuation to help you read accurately and take care when pronouncing unfamiliar words.

Autumn

The **water lilies** of summer are gone. They are no more.

Nothing remains but their umbrella leaves.

The **chrysanthemums** of Autumn are fading.

Their leaves are white with frost.

The beauty of the year is only a **solemn** memory.

Soon it will be winter and

Oranges turn gold and the **citrons** green.

> **water lilies:** water plants with large leaves
>
> **chrysanthemums:** brightly coloured flowers
>
> **solemn:** serious and sincere
>
> **citrons:** lemon-like fruits

2   In pairs, discuss whether or not you think 'Autumn' is an optimistic poem. Consider:

•   what is happening to the flowers

•   the meaning of the last two lines: is the narrator happy or sad that winter is coming?

Refer to specific lines from the poem to support your points and fully explore your views.

Language focus

In fiction, writers may deliberately choose the present tense to make the events they are describing seem immediate. This can convey a character's or narrator's excitement or concern, and draw the reader in.

Look at this sentence: 'The clouds are gathering above me.' The present tense verb 'are' means the reader 'experiences' the event at the same time as the narrator. It creates tension and emphasises the drama of the moment.

Continued

Writers may also use **conditional clauses** and **modal verbs** to suggest possible *future* events or outcomes, such as in the sentences: 'The clouds are gathering above me. If the storm breaks, it will mean disaster.' Here, the conditional clause (beginning 'If') alerts the reader to the possibility of something dangerous happening in the future. The modal verb 'will' suggests a definite outcome. The whole sentence has the effect of hinting at a terrible outcome, creating tension as the reader waits to find out what will happen.

Key words

conditional clause: part of a sentence that begins with 'if' or 'unless', suggesting something that could occur

modal verb: one of nine verbs used to show possibility – 'can', 'may', 'must', 'shall', 'will', 'could', 'might', 'should', 'would'

3 The poem 'The Turning Year' also deals with the theme of time passing: the feelings the narrator has as one year turns into the next.

Read the poem then, in pairs, compare it with 'Autumn'. Choose specific lines from both poems to explore the effect of:

a   the narrator's feelings about time passing

b   words connected with disappearance and cold

c   images connected to the natural world

d   use of the present tense alongside speculation about the future in the last two lines.

The Turning Year

Nightfall. Clouds scatter and vanish.
The sky is pure and cold.
If tonight I do not enjoy life to the full,
Next month, next year, who knows where I will be?

4 You are now going to write a short poem in the style of Su Tung P'o. Think of a title for your poem, then remind yourself of the language techniques Su Tung P'o uses and the voice of his narrators.

Your poem should:

- be 4–8 lines long

- be set at a specific time of year

- use words and images connected with nature

- be written in the present tense

- end with some speculation about the future to create a particular effect.

Peer assessment

Read each other's poems and give your partner feedback.

- Is their opening line effective – does it quickly convey the mood of the poem?

- How effective is the ending – do the last lines have a particular impact on you?

---

5 Writers create different voices depending on the audience, purpose and topic they are exploring, but poets often have a more distinctive voice – their writing has an individual tone and attitude.

In pairs, read Su Tung P'o's poem 'The End of the Year' on the next page, then discuss it.

a Is this is an optimistic poem or not?

b What similarities does this poem have with 'Autumn' and 'The Turning Year'?

c What have you learnt about the themes and voice of this poet from the three poems?

The End of the Year

When a year has gone, how will you ever find it again?

I wonder where it has gone, this year that is ended?

Certainly someplace far beyond the horizon.

It is gone like a river which flows to the East,

And empties into the sea without hope of return.

We leave the bygone year without regret.

Will we leave so carelessly the years to come?

Everything passes, everything

Goes, and never looks back,

And we grow older and less strong.

6 Think back to the discussions you have had in this session, then write a paragraph giving your personal response to the poetry of Su Tung P'o. Explain what you did, or did not, enjoy about the poems and how they made you feel.

Summary checklist

- ☐ I can read poetry aloud accurately and with confidence.
- ☐ I understand how a poet uses language and grammatical techniques to explore themes and create effects.
- ☐ I can write a short poem in a particular style, using appropriate language and structural features.
- ☐ I can write a personal response to a selection of poems by one writer.

> # 4.2 Making the most of time

In this session, you will:

- explore the effect of images and language choices in a poem
- consider how a poem's structure can be used to convey meaning
- discuss how personal beliefs can affect interpretations of a poem
- write a poem using genre features.

Getting started

There are many ways to describe people's attitude towards life. For example, 'looking on the bright side' means to be optimistic about a situation. How many other words and phrases can you think of to describe positive or negative views about life? Discuss your ideas in pairs.

'To Make Much of Time'

One of the challenges of reading older texts is understanding the language and references to different times and cultures. Read the opening **stanzas** of the poem 'To Make Much of Time' by Robert Herrick. In these lines, the narrator is addressing young people and making a point about the passing of time.

Key word

stanza: a group of lines of poetry, forming a unit

To Make Much of Time

Gather ye rosebuds while ye may,
Old Time is still a-flying;
And this same flower that smiles today
Tomorrow will be dying.

The glorious lamp of heaven, the sun,
The higher he's a-getting,
The sooner will his race be run,
And nearer he's to setting.

ye = can mean 'the' or 'you'

Old Time = a **personification** of time as an old man

setting = the sun going down at the end of the day

1   In pairs, use the picture and learner's notes on the language to help you discuss the following questions:

   a   Why does the narrator advise readers to gather rosebuds while they can?

   b   What impression do you get of Old Time from the lines?

   c   What connects the images of the flower and the setting sun?

2   The poet uses metaphors of a flower and the sun to suggest that time passes quickly: even when things seem young and strong, they are gradually dying.

   What other metaphors could you use to describe the passing of time? In pairs, make a list of natural or human-made objects and events that could represent the passing of time.

Now read the last two stanzas of the poem. In the first two lines, the narrator says that youth is the best part of life, because people are 'warmer' – they have more energy.

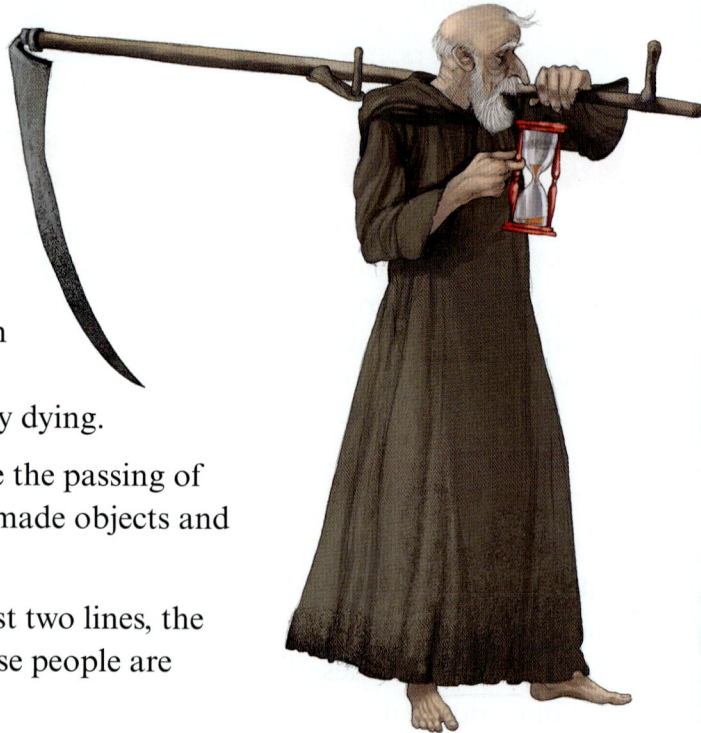

That age is best which is the first,
When youth and blood are warmer;
But being **spent**, the worse, and worst
Times still **succeed the former**.

Then be not **coy**, but use your time,
And while ye may, **go marry**;
For having lost but once your **prime**,
You may forever **tarry**.

spent: used up

succeed the former: come after the first part

coy: shy

go marry: unite; spend time with others

prime: the best part

tarry: wait

3 Write answers to the following questions.

   a In these stanzas, what advice does the narrator give about getting older?

   b How does the advice in the last stanza link to the title?

   c How effectively do you think the final line summarises the advice given in the poem?

   d How effectively does the title summarise the poem's message?

4 The structure of the poem helps to convey the poet's meaning. In pairs, read all four stanzas to each other, focusing on the rhyme and rhythm of the poem. Then make notes on:

   a how the regular rhyme and rhythm reflect ideas about time moving on

   b how each stanza contains a positive idea followed by a negative one, and the effect of this.

Carpe diem poetry

'To Make Much of Time' is an example of a *carpe diem* poem. This Latin phrase means 'seize the day' – make the most of your time right now. The article below discusses this type of poem.

Carpe diem poetry: inspiring the young?

Anyone who uses social media will have seen posts that are meant to inspire readers: they have beautiful pictures and words encouraging you to 'Keep going!' or 'Live life to the full!'. In literature, *carpe diem* poems give a similar message. They remind us to do things now, rather than putting them off to another day. How people react to *carpe diem* poems often reflects their own attitudes towards life. Some people are optimists – in the popular metaphor, they have a 'glass half full' attitude. Such people find *carpe diem* poems inspiring. But others are pessimists – they have a 'glass half empty' attitude towards life. These people would see these poems as a bit bleak or threatening, particularly the images of things dying, as if the poet is reminding us that life will come to an end all too soon.

5   In small groups, discuss:

- what the 'glass half full' and 'glass half empty' metaphor means

- your reactions to 'To Make Much of Time' – whether you found it inspiring

- your own attitude to life and how this might have influenced your reaction to the poem.

Make sure everyone contributes to the discussion, and fully explore any points of disagreement.

6   You are going to write a *carpe diem* poem aimed at teenagers. Remember that this type of poem:

- advises the reader to make the most of their time

- contains a metaphor to represent the passing of time

- uses positive and negative ideas.

Write your poem in modern standard English. Choose language and metaphors carefully to make an impact on your reader. Choose an appropriate title.

Think carefully about the structure of your poem: will you include rhyme or a regular rhythm? Your finished poem should be no more than 16 lines but you can choose how many stanzas to include. The final line should make a point clearly to the reader.

Writing tip

When writing short poems, start by thinking of a metaphor that sums up the main idea you want to express. If possible, read some other *carpe diem* poems to get some ideas for metaphors and to broaden the vocabulary and language you use in your poetry writing.

Self-assessment

Assess the effectiveness of your poem.

- Does the title introduce the message of the poem well?

- Is the final line strong enough – does it give the reader clear advice?

Summary checklist

- ☐ I can explain the effect of images and language choices in an older poem.
- ☐ I can analyse how structure is used to convey a poem's meaning.
- ☐ I can contribute effectively to a discussion about personal responses to a poem.
- ☐ I can write a poem incorporating specific features of the genre.

> 4.3 The tribe that time forgot

In this session, you will:

- give a personal reaction to an informative article
- identify meaning and bias in a text
- justify your opinions on a topic
- write and perform a persuasive speech.

Getting started

How would you feel if you did not have access to computers and phones? What would be the benefits and disadvantages? Discuss your ideas in pairs.

The tribe that time forgot

The article on the next page describes the lifestyle of the Baduy, a tribe that lives in the hills of Indonesia. Although they are only 120 kilometres from the capital city, Jakarta, they live an isolated life.

Outside world still a mystery to tribe that time forgot

The Baduy, who are estimated to number somewhere between 5000 and 8000 people, live in almost complete **seclusion**, observing customs that forbid using soap, riding vehicles or wearing shoes.

In the shadow of Mount Kendeng, the Baduy people cling to their way of life. The long list of **taboos** often appear to make their lives tough. School education, glass, nails, footwear and rearing four-legged animals are among some of things forbidden to the Baduy.

'There is no education. Going to the field is an education for them,' said Boedhihartono, of the University of Indonesia, who has studied the Baduy for years.

Their society is divided into an outer zone of villages and an inner heartland of three villages. Baduy who break the rules are banished to the outer zone.

Members of the inner zone of about 800 people, or 40 families, dress in white, as opposed to the black **attire** worn in the outer zone, and they follow the Baduy traditions much more strictly.

Foreigners are allowed to visit the outer zone but are limited to a few nights, sleeping on bamboo mats in villages at night.

Leaders from the inner Baduy sometimes pay surprise visits to make sure their outer-zone **compatriots** are not breaking too many taboos. They sometimes **confiscate** radios and other things from the modern world.

But it is difficult to keep all things at bay. On a recent trip, some Baduy children had **forsaken** traditional wear, one wearing a blue Italian football shirt.

'Even in the centre, they already know money,' said Boedhihartono, who has over several years developed what he describes as 'a sort of friendship' with the Baduy.

Asked if they knew much of the outside world, he said: 'Of course not really, except if they come to my house, they watch the TV.'

---

seclusion: being away from other people
taboos: forbidden things
attire: clothing

compatriots: people who live in the same place
confiscate: take away
forsaken: abandoned, given up

1　How do you react to the information about the Baduy's lifestyle? Make notes using quotations from the text.

2　What is the writer's attitude towards the Baduy's way of life? Does this article show evidence of bias? In pairs, discuss:

- the type of information the writer does and does not give about the tribe – for example, does the writer mention any positive aspects of the Baduy lifestyle?

- whose views are and are not represented in the article

- what is implied in the last paragraph and the effect of ending the article with this information.

Reading tip

The structural choices a writer makes can reveal their attitudes to the topic. In particular, the last part of text often reveals a writer's ideas and opinions, as they want to leave their reader with a strong final impression.

3　Modern technology can make our lives simpler and easier. But some communities around the world avoid it because they believe such developments are a negative influence on society. What do you think?

In pairs, make a list of eight things that you believe the world would be better without. These might be small items that annoy you, technology you find frustrating or more serious things that have caused people harm. Discuss your list, giving reasons for your choices, then choose *one* object each you would 'uninvent' if you could.

4　You are going to write a two-minute speech about the object you would like to uninvent. The purpose of your speech is to persuade the class to support your choice.

Start by putting the points you want to make and the reasons you will give into a mind map. Then choose the best way of sequencing your points. Remember, it is a good idea to build up to your most convincing point.

Think carefully about your audience – how can you adapt your speech to have the biggest impact? And remember that the type of object you have chosen will affect the tone of your speech – will yours be light-hearted and entertaining, or serious?

Try to include some of the following features of persuasive texts:

- hyperbole (exaggerated statements)

- rhetorical questions (questions designed to make you think rather than requiring an answer)

- exclamations (comments expressing strong emotions such as surprise or anger)

- statistics (facts based on numbers and data)

- triples (three words used together in a list for persuasive effect)

- emotive language (language designed to appeal to a reader's emotions)

- repetition (using the same word or phrase more than once for effect)

- figurative language (words and phrases used not with their basic meaning but with a more imaginative meaning to create a special effect; figurative language techniques include simile, metaphor and personification)

- direct address (speaking directly to any audience using pronouns such as 'you')

- imperatives (a word or phrase styled as an order or command).

5 Rehearse your speech, considering any visual aids that might be helpful, and how you can use gesture and variations in the volume and speed of your voice. Remember to plan *how* you will speak as well as what you will say.

Finally, give your speech to the class as confidently as possible.

Think about the writing and delivery of your speech.
- Which parts of the process did you find most challenging and why?
- How could you overcome these challenges next time?

Summary checklist

- ☐ I can give a personal response to an informative article.
- ☐ I can identify and interpret meanings and bias in a non-fiction article.
- ☐ I can write and perform an effective speech using a range of persuasive techniques.
- ☐ I can justify my opinion in a discussion.

> 4.4 The time tornado

In this session, you will:

- discuss genre features in relation to a story
- explore the structure and effect of a story opening
- consider how verb choices convey action, pace and atmosphere
- write an effective story opening.

Listening tip

When making notes from spoken texts, make sure you identify all the key information. Do not try to note down everything; instead, use a table or bullet points to briefly record the essential information. Remember that key information is likely to be directly linked to the main focus of the topic.

Getting started

In pairs, discuss the openings of stories you have read. Which ones did you like best? Why?

1 Listen to the audio, in which the speaker explains the features of the fantasy genre. As you listen, make a list of the features of this genre.

Tanglewreck

Now read the opening of a fantasy novel called *Tanglewreck* by Jeanette Winterson.

Extract 1

The Time Tornado

At six forty-five one summer morning, a red London bus was crossing Waterloo Bridge.

A group of school children, sitting at the back, were copying each other's homework when one of them looked out of the window, across the river to Cleopatra's Needle, and saw something very strange.

The boy elbowed his friend. The dark finger of ancient Egypt was pointing towards the sky as it always did, but today the tip was glowing bright red, as it had when it was new and painted and glorious, four thousand years ago, in the Temple of the Sun.

'Look,' said the boy, 'look!'

Riding the river as though it were a road was a **phalanx** of **chariots** and horsemen.

The white horses were pulled up, the troops stood at ease, and above the kneeling priests was the **Pharaoh** himself.

Other people turned to stare and the bus driver slowed down, though he did not quite stop; he seemed to be hovering over Time.

In the slowed-down silence no one spoke and nothing moved – except for the river, which to all observation was running backwards.

Then, from downstream, there was a sudden terrible crack, like the sky breaking. A cone of wind hit the bus, knocking it sideways over the bridge and shattering glass across the seats where the children were sitting.

The bus should have crashed down into the river, but instead the wind whirled through the punched-in windows and lifted the bus high above the bridge.

A great wave of water swelled up against the bridge, battering the concrete with such force that part of the wall was torn away.

As the tidal wave slammed back down on to the water, the river resumed its normal flow. At the same second the bus spun crazily into the line of chariots. On impact, bus, chariots and horsemen vanished, leaving nothing behind but traces of red-gold sun on the surface of the water.

A few days later police found an exercise book floating on the **Thames**; the name printed in the front of the book identified it as belonging to one of the boys on the bus. The pages had thickened, and the writing inside was not English, but signs of long-legged birds and half-turned figures.

The bus and its passengers were never found.

It was the first of the Time Tornadoes.

Cleopatra's Needle: a stone monument given to the UK by Egypt

phalanx: a group of people moving close together

chariot: an ancient two-wheeled vehicle drawn by horses

pharaoh: a ruler in ancient Egypt

Thames: the river running through London

2 Work in pairs. Which features of the fantasy genre you noted in Activity 1 can you identify in the extract?

3 The opening of any story is an important part of its structure. Writers may use their first chapter to introduce main characters and problems, or they may focus on creating a sense of mystery or introducing a key theme.

Reread the extract from *Tanglewreck*, then complete the following tasks.

a Explain what you think a 'Time Tornado' might be.

b Write an analysis of the 'shape' of the first chapter – which moments are calm and which are dramatic? What is the overall effect of this structure?

c List all the mysterious events and characters in the extract. What effect do they have on the reader?

Language focus

Verbs are usually used to show action, but they are also effective when describing events and characters. Careful verb choices can convey important shades of meaning. For example, verbs such as 'looked' or 'walked' suggest a fairly calm state of being. However, more dramatic verbs, such as 'hurled' or 'yelled', not only show action, but also suggest something about the personality and emotion of the character or scene.

Writers may change the verbs they choose to create certain effects. Look at this example:

- It was so strange. One moment, we were <u>chatting</u> by the river as the sun <u>looked</u> down, then without warning, the sky <u>darkened</u>, the rain <u>spat</u>, and the river violently <u>lashed</u> at the people in the rowing boat.

Notice how the verbs 'chatting' and 'looked' give an impression of peace and very little movement. This is contrasted with the colour and anger suggested by 'darkened', 'spat' and 'lashed', which create a more threatening effect. The shift between quality of verbs gives a sudden sense of drama and suggests the theme of the piece – that events can change unexpectedly.

4   Write a paragraph analysing the effect of verb choices in the opening of *Tanglewreck*. Carefully select examples to explain the shift between calmness and drama, and comment on the effect of these choices.

5   Using the opening of *Tanglewreck* as a model, write your own story opening of about 250 words involving a Time Tornado. Set it in your own country and choose which period or characters from history to include. Choose effective verbs to structure your opening, showing the shift from one mood to another. Use appropriate strategies to ensure your spelling is accurate.

Peer assessment

Swap your story opening with a partner and give each other feedback.

- How effective are their opening sentences – do they help you picture the scene?

- Does the structure of their story show a good balance between moods, such as calmness and dramatic action?

- Do their verb choices vividly convey the events taking place?

Summary checklist

☐ I can make notes on the features of a genre, then identify those features in a story opening.

☐ I can analyse the effect of a story opening.

☐ I understand how verb choices can convey action and establish a change in mood and pace.

☐ I can write an effective story opening, using structural and grammatical features to show a shift in pace.

> 4.5 The visitor

In this session, you will:

- consider the effect of withholding information from readers
- explore the methods a writer uses to portray a mysterious character
- discuss how a story might develop based on events so far
- write a chapter containing mysterious events.

Getting started

In pairs, make a list of mysterious characters in books you have read. Discuss what makes them mysterious and what they do as the stories develop.

In the second chapter of *Tanglewreck*, a new, mysterious character called Abel Darkwater arrives at an old house.

Extract 2

The Visitor

At 4:30 p.m. precisely, Abel Darkwater drove through the gates of the great house called Tanglewreck.

Abel Darkwater was never late – unless he intended to be; and his watch was never wrong – unless he wanted it to be.

Some people are always short of time, but Abel Darkwater had all the time in the world – well, *nearly* all of it – and it was the nearly that was the problem, and the reason why he had come to Tanglewreck.

He steered the big car up the long ragged driveway. He glanced at the round green dials on the dashboard. The **luminous** clock assured him that he was **punctual**, and the Age-Gauge steadied its hands at 1588, the year Tanglewreck had been built.

The Age-Gauge worked on echoes of time. Abel Darkwater knew that all time is always present, but buried layer by layer under what people call Now. Today lies on top of yesterday, and yesterday lies on top of the day before, and so on down the layers of history, until the layers are so thick that the voices underneath are muffled to whispers. Abel Darkwater listened to those whispers and he understood what they said.

Now he was at Tanglewreck, and the house was telling him the beginning of its own past – the day when it was a young house new-made. When Now was Then and Then was Now. He was curious to hear more, but he had come here today on business, and he must not keep that business waiting.

He pulled up outside the house, and switched off the engine. He heaved himself slowly out of his car, and consulted his heavy gold pocket watch: the hour hand marked four. The minute hand thirty-five past the hour. The second hand moved swiftly from forty to fifty. The fourth hand, in red, like a warning, pointed towards eleven o'clock. Abel Darkwater looked up, following the direction of his watch. Sure enough, there was a face at the window.

luminous: bright or shining
punctual: on time

1   Use the most appropriate strategy to find and make notes on all the references to time in this extract and the overall effect they create.

2   The introduction of Abel Darkwater and the setting of the house Tanglewreck both create a sense of mystery, as the writer withholds information about them.

In pairs, discuss what the writer *does* and *does not* tell the reader about the character and setting. How do these structural decisions contribute to the sense of mystery? Be precise in your explanations.

3   The language, punctuation and grammatical patterns in the extract build an interesting description of Abel Darkwater.

Look at the sentence below, which uses two similar clauses separated by a semi-colon:

Abel Darkwater was never late – unless he intended to be; and his watch was never wrong – unless he wanted it to be.

In your pairs, analyse the effect of the patterns of language, punctuation and grammar used here. What impression do they create of Abel Darkwater?

4   Write two paragraphs about the way the writer presents Abel Darkwater in this extract. You should comment on:

•   the **connotations** of his name

•   his ability to understand time

•   the information you are given about the Age-Gauge and his pocket watch

•   the way the writer uses language and grammatical patterns.

5   In small groups, discuss what you think might happen next. Remember to take turns so everyone contributes, and respect each other's ideas. In particular, consider:

•   why Abel might be visiting Tanglewreck

•   what the interior of the house might look like

•   who the 'face at window' could be and what connection they might have with Abel

•   whether the action will involve conflict.

Reading tip

When analysing the effect of grammatical patterns in a story, consider how they relate to character or theme. For example, if sentences are short and repetitive, they might reflect the tension felt by the main character.

Key word

connotations: the ideas or feelings associated with a word

6 Now write the next chapter of *Tanglewreck*, developing the sense of mystery. Describe what happens when Abel enters the house, and develop the new character – the face at the window.

Write in a similar style to the extracts you have read, considering language, structure and grammatical patterns. Write approximately 350 words in good, fluent handwriting.

Peer assessment

Swap your writing with a partner and give them feedback.

- Have they created enough mystery to make you want to carry on reading?

- How interesting was their use and development of the face at the window?

7 Edit your draft, taking your partner's feedback into consideration. Proofread your writing, checking your spelling carefully. Remember to use your knowledge of word families as well as a dictionary to make sure your work is accurate.

Summary checklist

- [ ] I understand the effect of withholding information in a story.
- [ ] I can analyse the techniques a writer uses to make a character seem mysterious.
- [ ] I can contribute effectively to a discussion on what might happen next in a story.
- [ ] I can write a chapter of a mystery story using appropriate structural, language and grammatical features.

› 4.6 Into the future

In this session, you will:

- explore the impact of variations in speech
- practise group work and discussion skills
- consider how a writer creates an informal voice
- write in an informal voice.

Getting started

How do you think schools will change in the future? In pairs, discuss what a typical lesson might be like in the year 2060, then share your ideas with the class.

Ways of speaking

People vary the way they speak depending on the situation. Where and when you are talking, the topic and your audience can all influence how you speak. Read the two **transcripts** on the next page, which are based on the question in the Getting started activity. In the first, Ahmed is talking to his friend. In the second one, he is explaining his thoughts to his teacher in front of the class.

Key word

transcript: a written version of a speech or conversation

🎧 32 Ahmed and Abeed

ABEED   What do you think then? What will it be like in 2060?

AHMED   That's hard to answer. Er . . . there'll probably be more computers in classrooms. Maybe we won't need to write with pens. That would be good actually. I prefer typing – I'm quicker at it than writing, so yeah – more computers and no pens. I hope that happens, although I'll be nearly 50 by then and so I'll have left school! So yeah – if I have kids myself, they might not know how to hold a pen!

🎧 33 Ahmed and Mr Ganem

MR GANEM   Ahmed, can you summarise your thoughts for the class please?

AHMED   Yes, Mr Ganem. Abeed and I think that there'll be significant changes in technology. For instance, it is likely there will be many more computers in classrooms by 2060 and maybe some of the traditional ways of writing will not be as common. I think this will be helpful for many learners who prefer typing their work.

1   Work in pairs.

    a   Identify the differences in the way Ahmed speaks in each transcript.

    b   Discuss how these differences might affect the meaning of what he is saying. Which one seems a more serious and sincere view?

    c   Analyse the impact of these variations on the two audiences – how are listeners likely to react to the way they are spoken to?

A bright future

Read the following article from an online magazine for young people.
In it, the writer predicts how the world will change by 2060.

34

The future is bright

Where will you be in 2060? You've probably never thought about
it. In fact, you probably don't even think about where you'll be
next week, do you? But for a minute, come with me into the future
and I'll show you what you'll be doing many years from now.

1   No more holidays. Who wants to travel for hours? Boring!
    Instead, a travel agent will **implant** a memory of a holiday
    into your brain, so you can have all those great memories
    without having to leave home. Enjoy Mars!

2   No more school. I like teachers, but by 2060, your phone
    will be able to design the perfect individual lesson. You
    can decide when you start and finish, so no more early
    mornings. In fact, you can stay in bed and learn . . .

3   No more disease. Developments in medicine mean that
    you can live forever. Like a car, you will be regularly checked
    and repaired by your doctor. It might not be cheap, but you
    can't put a price on health!

implant: insert
into the body

Speaking tip

If you are the
chairperson,
make sure you
encourage all
group members
to give their
opinions. Use
your judgement
to decide when to
move on to a new
topic, and help
the group come
to a final decision.

2   In groups, discuss the predictions in the article. Consider:

- what the benefits and disadvantages of each prediction
  would be

- whether these changes would make the world a
  better place

- which one of the predictions would you like to come true
  and why.

Before you start, agree on the roles you will take in the
discussion. For example, someone may act as **chairperson** and
someone else may be in charge of taking notes. During the
discussion, make sure you contribute your own ideas, as well
as taking turns to speak.

Key word

chairperson:
someone who is
in overall charge
of a discussion or
debate

- What was your most important contribution to the discussion?
- Are there any roles you would like to try out next time?

3   As a group, explain to the class which prediction you chose and why. Plan what you will say so that each group member contributes.

When other members of your group are speaking, think about the variations in their speech – how does it differ between group work and class explanation?

4   'The future is bright' article uses informal language and a conversational voice, as if the writer is talking directly to the reader in a friendly way.

Write an analysis of how the writer has created this voice. Identify the use and effect of:

- punctuation choices
- the use of the second person pronoun 'you'
- the range of sentence types
- repetition.

5   Write two more predictions about 2060. Use similar grammar and punctuation choices to those in the article to convey an informal voice for an audience of people your own age.

> **Writing tip**
>
> Develop the ability to decide how much to plan before writing. Some pieces of writing need careful decisions about structure, but in situations such as exams, planning might be briefer. Bear in mind that practising the skill of 'writing as you go' is a very useful one when time is short.

> **Summary checklist**
>
> ☐ I understand how variations in speech have a different impact on audiences.
> ☐ I can work effectively in a group, contributing ideas and listening to others.
> ☐ I can explain the methods a writer uses to create a particular voice.
> ☐ I can use language, punctuation and grammar techniques to write in an informal voice.

Check your progress

Answer the following questions.

1 Note down two ideas that could help you to read aloud an unseen poem as accurately as possible.

2 What is *carpe diem* poetry and how might different readers react to such poems?

3 Write a list of tips for learners for writing a persuasive speech.

4 Using examples, explain how writers create mystery in opening chapters.

5 'A key method in creating mystery is to withhold information from the reader.' Using your own words, explain what this means.

6 Explain some factors that influence the way people speak.

Project

Imagine you have been given the power to shape the future. Rather than adults deciding what happens, *you* can.

In groups, prepare a presentation in which you explain four things that you would like to change about the world. They must be things that will make the lives of ordinary people better.

Start by discussing a whole range of different ideas and making lists of possible benefits and disadvantages of each idea. Gradually reduce these ideas to a list of four and consider how each idea could be carried out – what would you need to do to ensure it happened?

Prepare your talk by deciding what you will say and how you will structure the presentation. In particular, think about how you will introduce and conclude it. Make sure everybody contributes.

For each idea, you should explain:

- why you have chosen it
- how it will benefit people
- how you could make it happen.

Your presentation should last at least ten minutes. You can decide whether to use visual aids.

5 ▶ That's entertainment

In this unit, you will read entertaining texts, including a comedy play and an account of a fantastic achievement. You will also explore issues about fame and music, and debate ideas around the use of animals to entertain people.

> 5.1 Leaving Jamaica

In this session, you will:

- read an unseen drama script
- identify features of the comedy genre
- explore the importance of performance in creating comedy
- consider the way asides are used to convey character and situation.

Getting started

In pairs, discuss books, plays and films that make you laugh. What is it about the characters and situations that you find amusing?

EMPIRE WINDRUSH

Small Island

Small Island is a **dramatic comedy** based on a novel by Andrea Levy. It follows the lives of Gilbert and Hortense, two Jamaicans who travel to England to start a new life. In real life, many people made this journey after the British government invited people to emigrate there from the Caribbean. They became known as the 'Windrush' generation, after a ship that carried one of the first groups there in 1948.

In the scene below, the initial **comedic problem** is introduced – both characters want a better life. They use their creativity to come up with a plan, but in doing so, they create another issue – they will have to endure each other's company! Gilbert is an energetic and likeable character who entertains the audience with his lively, positive attitude. Hortense amuses the audience because she is a little pretentious – she wants to be seen as more important than she really is.

1   Read the play in pairs, taking care to speak the dialogue accurately and confidently. Remember to read ahead where possible.

Extract 1

GILBERT *enters. He is holding a flyer in his hand.*
HORTENSE *goes to him.*

GILBERT	You see this? The Empire Windrush, sailing for England. Two months' time. Man, I wish I could be on that ship.
HORTENSE	Perhaps you could be.
GILBERT	You seen how much it cost?
HORTENSE	I will lend you the money.
GILBERT	What, sorry?
	She doesn't reply.
	I don't understand.
HORTENSE	**Prudence**. Something my uncle taught me. A little of my wages every week.
	You can pay me back.
GILBERT	Oh, I surely would. What I don't understand, is why you would lend me the money?

Key words

dramatic comedy: a play that contains elements of comedy, such as a happy ending and funny events

comedic problem: a challenge that characters in comedy face – often a situation or character that stands in the way of happiness

Speaking tip

Dialogue often contains informal and non-standard phrases, to make it sound realistic. When reading dialogue aloud, pay particular attention to the words and phrases, and take the time to understand what they mean and how the character would speak them.

prudence: cautiousness; thinking about the future

HORTENSE	So you can go to England. I will lend you the money, we will be married and you can send for me to come to England when you have a place for me to live.
GILBERT	Whoa! Just say that again because I think me ears playing a trick on me.
HORTENSE	A single woman cannot travel on her own – it would not be respectable. But a married woman might go anywhere she pleases. Marry me, and go to England.
	GILBERT *leaves* HORTENSE *and goes to stand alone.*
GILBERT (*to audience and himself*)	This is a tough one. Man, this woman don't even like me as far as I can tell. My face seem to distress her, my jokes confuse her. She surely thinks she's better than me. But England.
HORTENSE (*to audience and herself*)	I cannot be the fool who is left behind again. It is better that I go to England. England will give me a fine welcome because of my pale skin and my education. England is my golden life.
GILBERT (*to audience and himself*)	I'm done with this small island. I seen too much of the world now. I stay here, I become one of those big-talk men, small coins jangling in my ragged pockets even as I tell my tales. How I ever be a lawyer if I stay here?
HORTENSE (*to audience and herself*)	In England I will have a smart front door and I will ring the bell – ding-a-ling, ding-a-ling. I will be a teacher, greeted with manners and respect. And no one . . . no one will feel sorry for I.

EMPIRE WINDRUSH DOCKED HERE AT TILBURY JUNE 22ND 1948

'LONDON ISN'T LIKE WE VILLAGE DIRT ROAD, YOU KNOW LEELA IT A PARISH OF A PASTURE-LAN' WHAT GROWN CRISSCROSS STREETS, AN' THEY LIE DOWN TO MY DOOR' JAMES BERRY

2 Listen to the audio recording – an interview with someone discussing the features of the comedy genre. Make notes on these features, then identify which ones you can find in Extract 1.

3 Successful comedy relies partly on performance and delivery – the way lines are said and how characters move and react. This means it can be hard to 'see' comedy in a script.

In pairs, experiment with different ways of performing the dialogue that starts with Hortense saying *So you can go to England*. Use your voice, movement and drama to bring out the humour of Hortense's bold plan and Gilbert's astonishment.

Language focus

In a play, there is usually no narrator to describe and explain characters' thoughts. Instead, a playwright relies on words and actions to express such thoughts and feelings. One way writers indicate these is through a structural device called an **aside**. This is where a character expresses a thought aloud with the implication that other characters do not hear them. Look at this example:

MAHSA	Can you give the money back next week?
DARAB	Of course! (*aside*) What am I going to do? There's no way I can find the money before then!

The aside gives the audience extra information – that Darab cannot afford to repay Mahsa – and sets up possible conflict later in the play. Asides invite the audience to see things from a particular character's point of view, sharing their private concerns, which can establish a sense of sympathy between audience and character.

Asides also contribute to another feature of plays – **dramatic irony**. This is when the audience knows more than the characters on stage. Here, after hearing the aside, the audience knows that although Mahsa is expecting her money back next week, she is going to be disappointed. Dramatic irony can create effects such as humour or tension.

Listening tip

Once you have made brief notes from an audio source, try to organise them logically – perhaps using different colours to highlight key information or even rewriting them in a more visually appealing way. This will help you to revise and remember information.

Key words

aside: a remark by a character in a play that is heard by the audience, but not by the other characters on stage

dramatic irony: when an audience's awareness of a situation is different to that of the characters on stage

4   Reread the extract from *Small Island* then write a brief analysis of the effect that the asides have – indicated by the words *(to audience and himself/herself)*. Explain:

- what they reveal about the character's motivations for travelling to England

- how Gilbert thinks Hortense views him and your reaction to it (whether or not you find this amusing)

- the different effects created by the asides

- the effect of placing these asides later in the structure of this scene.

Summary checklist

☐ I can read an unseen dramatic comedy accurately, reading ahead when necessary.

☐ I understand the genre features of comedy.

☐ I can explain how comedy is conveyed through words and actions in a dramatic performance.

☐ I can explain how asides are used to convey character and create effects in drama.

> # 5.2 Arriving in England

In this session, you will:

- read and perform a comedy scene

- explore how contrast is used to create humour

- respond to familiar situations and stereotypes in a play extract

- write your own comedy scene.

Getting started

In pairs, discuss comedy shows and books that feature pairs of characters. What qualities and attitudes do each of the characters show? How do you react to them? How is the comedy created in the interactions between the characters?

Below is another scene from *Small Island*. It takes place in London, where Gilbert is renting a room from a woman called Queenie. Hortense has travelled by ship from Jamaica, and Gilbert is supposed to meet her. Part of the comedy in the scene comes from Gilbert's disorganised manner and his desire to please Hortense. The gap between what Hortense expects England to be and her disappointment in the room creates humour for some readers, while for others it is also a reminder of life's difficulties.

Extract 2

A grey, starkly realistic world.

A small room at the top of QUEENIE's *house. A single bed, a small table and two chairs – one of which has a broken leg and rests on an old book. There is a gas fire and an armchair. In one corner there is a gas ring, a sink and a kettle. A very small window looks out onto rooftops. It is a late afternoon in November and the sky is already growing dim.*

GILBERT, *fully-dressed, is asleep on the bed. Downstairs, the front-door bell rings. After a moment it rings again.* GILBERT *suddenly sits up.*

GILBERT   Oh, no.

He checks his watch.

No! No, no, no!

The bell rings again as GILBERT *frantically pulls on his shoes and fastens the loose buttons on his shirt.*

No!

GILBERT *rushes from the room, tripping over his not-quite-done-up shoelaces, and we hear the sound of him running down the stairs. We hear his voice joining those of the others, loud at first and then quiet.*

(Off) Not much further now.

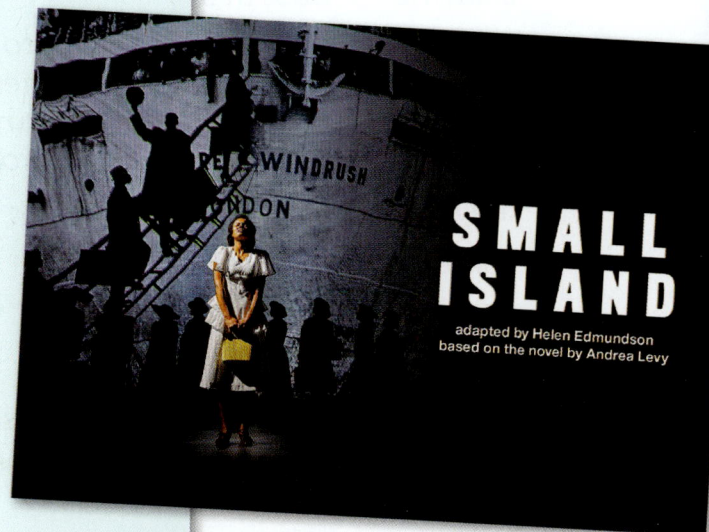

SMALL ISLAND

adapted by Helen Edmundson
based on the novel by Andrea Levy

More footsteps. GILBERT *appears in the doorway and holds the door open for* HORTENSE *to enter. She is dressed in a* pristine *white coat with the white hat and gloves she wore for her wedding. She has a handbag over her arm.*

Here we are.

HORTENSE *stands in the doorway, taking in the room. She is disorientated, shocked, inwardly afraid, but she is determined to cover it. He looks at her, smiling nervously. She swallows.*

HORTENSE   Well show me the rest.

She looks at him and he stares at her.

Show me the rest, nah. I am tired from the long, long journey. The other rooms, GILBERT. The ones you say you so busy making nice for me that you forget to come and meet me at the dock.

GILBERT   But . . . that is it.

HORTENSE   I beg your pardon?

GILBERT   This is it. This is the room I am living.

HORTENSE *stares around the room again in shocked silence.*

HORTENSE   Just this?

She suddenly has to sit down on the edge of a chair so that her legs don't give way. GILBERT *swings his arms as though to suggest how spacious the room is.*

GILBERT   Yes. This is it.

HORTENSE   Just this?

pristine: perfect, as new

1   Read the scene in pairs.

a   Read through the scene once slowly, taking time to understand the **stage directions** and what the characters are doing as they speak.

b   Then perform the scene as confidently as you can in order to bring out the characters' personalities, attitudes and emotions.

Key words

stage directions: words in a script that explain what is happening on stage or tell the actors how to move and speak

Speaking tip

Before performing, think about the emotions of the characters at different points in the scene, imagining what their attitude or concerns might be. This will help you decide how to use and vary your voice and movement to show your character's feelings and emotions.

Self-assessment

Think about the way you performed the scene.

- Did you speak confidently in your character's voice, effectively conveying their personality?

- How effectively did you use your voice – was there enough variation to convey your character's emotions?

2   **Contrast** is an important structural device in plays. In *Small Island*, the two characters contrast with each other in both their physical differences and in their opposing attitudes. Contrasts like this are often used to create comedy.

Look at Extract 2 again, then write a 150-word analysis of how Gilbert and Hortense are presented here to create humorous contrasts. Consider:

- how they dress, move and behave

- their reactions to the room

- the **quickfire dialogue** and what it suggests about their relationship.

Key words

contrast: placing two characters or things together in order to highlight their differences

quickfire dialogue: a rapid exchange of lines between characters

3   Comedy often focuses on recognisable **stereotypes** of characters and situations. For example, most people will have overslept at some point, so the audience will **empathise** with Gilbert's panic at the start of the scene. Often the response to seeing and understanding such behaviour is laughter!

In groups, discuss your response to the following features of the scene – are they funny, or is your reaction to them more complicated? Take turns to explore your views thoroughly.

- the stereotype of the disorganised male
- the stereotype of the overdressed female
- the difference between Hortense's expectations and the reality of the room
- whether the scene is amusing or sad – or both.

4   Write your own comedy scene (about 250 words) involving two contrasting characters. Start by planning a scenario. For example, you could write about a brother and sister having a disagreement, or a scene in a shop where someone is returning a faulty phone.

Next, think about the differences between the characters and how you will show their voice through words and stage directions. Choose words carefully and use quickfire dialogue to indicate your characters' feelings.

Writing tip

Playwrights rely on stage directions to tell a story. Remember that many people will read scripts rather than see them performed on stage, so craft your stage directions so readers can picture the setting and the actions of the characters.

Summary checklist

- [ ] I can understand and perform a comedy scene from a play.
- [ ] I understand how playwrights use contrast to create humour.
- [ ] I can discuss and explain my reaction to stereotypes in a scene from a play.
- [ ] I can write an effective comedy scene, using contrast and dialogue for effect.

> 5.3 *The Boy Who Harnessed the Wind*

In this session, you will:

- consider the importance of titles
- explore structural patterns in an autobiography
- consider how figurative language adds layers of meaning and effect
- write a first-person account in a specific voice.

Getting started

In pairs, list the titles of some books you have read recently.
What effect do these titles have on you as a reader?
Which are the most interesting titles? Explain your ideas.

Key words

autobiography: a text in which the writer gives an account of their own life and experiences

prologue: an introductory section to a piece of writing

The Boy Who Harnessed the Wind

The Boy Who Harnessed the Wind is an entertaining **autobiography** of Malawian teenager William Kamkwamba. He built a windmill to generate electricity, which changed the lives of the people who lived in his village.

1 The title of a book is important – it is designed to summarise the story or intrigue the reader. Before reading the **prologue** from *The Boy Who Harnessed the Wind* by William Kamkwamba and Bryan Mealer, discuss the title in pairs. Consider:

- the effect of choosing the word 'boy' rather than using his name
- the connotations of the word 'harnessed'
- the overall impression the title creates of William
- the type of account you are led to expect.

38

The machine was ready. After so many months of preparation, the work was finally complete: The motor and blades were bolted and secured, the chain was **taut** and heavy with grease, and the tower stood steady in its legs. And although I'd barely slept the night before, I'd never felt so awake. My invention was complete. It appeared exactly as I'd seen it in my dreams.

News of my work had spread far and wide, and now people began to arrive. The traders in the market had watched it rise from a distance and they'd closed up their shops, while the truck drivers left their vehicles on the road. They'd crossed the valley toward my home, and now they gathered under the machine, looking up in wonder. I recognised their faces. These same men had teased me from the beginning, and still they whispered, even laughed.

Let them, I thought. It was time.

I pulled myself onto the tower's first rung and began to climb. The soft wood groaned under my weight as I reached the top, where I stood level with my creation. Its steel bones were **welded** and bent, and its plastic arms were blackened from fire.

I admired its other pieces: the bottle-cap washers, rusted tractor parts, and the old bicycle frame. Each one told its own story of discovery. Each piece had been lost and then found in a time of fear and hunger and pain. Together now, we were all being reborn.

In one hand I clutched a small **reed** that held a tiny lightbulb. I now connected it to a pair of wires that dangled from the machine, then prepared for the final step. Down below, the crowd cackled like hens.

'Quiet everyone,' someone said. 'Let's see how crazy this boy really is.'

Just then a strong gust of wind whistled through the rungs and pushed me into the tower. Reaching over, I unlocked the machine's spinning wheel and watched it begin to turn.

taut: stretched or pulled tight

welded: joined by heat

reed: a stalk

Slowly at first, then faster and faster, until the whole tower rocked back and forth. My knees turned to jelly, but I held on.

I pleaded in silence: *Don't let me down.*

Then I gripped the reed and wires and waited for the miracle of electricity. Finally, it came, a tiny flicker in my palm, and then a magnificent glow. The crowd gasped, and the children pushed for a better look.

'It's true!' someone said.

'Yes,' said another. 'The boy has done it. He has made electric wind!'

2   *The Boy Who Harnessed the Wind* is a story of triumph. Its structure is similar to many comedy texts. It includes:

   •   an ordinary setting

   •   a heroic character who succeeds by his own abilities

   •   the admiration of the hero by the community at the end.

   Write a summary of these structural patterns in relation to *The Boy Who Harnessed the Wind*. Use examples from the text and explain their overall effect – how does the reader react?

3   Autobiography is a type of non-fiction, but it is similar to fiction in that it is often carefully shaped and crafted to tell a story. For example, the prologue is a **flashforward** – it tells the reader how the story ends.

   In pairs, discuss the effect of the following structural choices:

   •   starting the text with a flashforward

   •   the contrast between William's hopes and fears about the machine and the doubts of the people in the crowd

   •   the use of tension and release.

> **Key word**
>
> **flashforward:** part of a story that describes a future event

Language focus

Figurative language, such as metaphor, simile and personification, helps readers to understand objects and feelings by offering a point of comparison. However, figurative language can also add extra layers of meaning to the object being described. Consider this example:

- As Jin walked into the room, the air crackled with electricity.

On one level, this metaphor simply helps the reader understand the excitement Jin's entrance creates. However, the use of electricity as a metaphor opens up other layers of meaning:

- As well as giving energy, electricity is a powerful force that also has the potential to cause harm.

- Electricity has the power to transform, changing situations and people permanently.

- Electricity is generated by human effort – a combination of natural products being harnessed and used by people.

These different, sometimes contradictory, meanings in the metaphor create a more complex and more interesting image of Jin and give a greater depth of character.

4   Write an analysis of the two uses of figurative language in the quotations from the extract. Explain the range of meanings they suggest and how they contribute to the overall effect of William's account:

    a   *together now, we were all being <u>reborn</u>*

    b   *the <u>miracle</u> of electricity.*

5   Imagine you are one of the villagers in the crowd, watching William try the machine for the first time. Write a 250-word account of what you see and feel in the voice of an adult who does not think the machine will work.

Start by planning the sequence of your account, using a tension-and-release structure. Choose language carefully, using figurative language and dialogue if you wish. Choose an effective title for your account.

Writing tip

Remember that contrast is an effective structural device in any account. Help the reader understand the range of feelings by including contrasting characters and opinions, or even between a character and the setting.

〉 5.4 K-pop

In this session, you will:

- explore two texts on similar themes
- consider the effect of organisational features in non-fiction
- discuss a range of responses to a text
- analyse how your own context affects your response to a text.

Getting started

In pairs, discuss new or unusual books and music that you know. How do your own previous experiences and views affect the way you react to new or different types of books and music?

K-pop idols

K-pop is a genre of music from South Korea. Read the non-fiction article below from the *Korea Times* by Dong Sun-hwa – an account of a young man trying to make a success of his music career.

How to be a K-pop idol:
A day in the life of an aspiring star juggling endless practice with school

- Jeon Sung-won's dreams of K-pop stardom see him practising up to 50 hours a week.

- With so many aspiring singers in South Korea, the probability of success is incredibly low.

Jeon Sung-won, 19, is a busy young man. On weekdays, he spends five hours after school taking vocal and piano lessons. On weekends and holidays, his practice begins at 10 am and continues until midnight.

It is exhausting. But Jeon cannot ease off, knowing how hard it will be to achieve his dream to be a K-pop star given the number of aspiring singers in South Korea, which is estimated to be more than a million.

This is why most South Korean parents are reluctant to support their children's dreams.

'My parents convinced me to give up the dream initially,' Jeon says. 'But I persuaded them, telling them how desperate I was to work in the industry. In the future, I want to be a successful singer and pay my parents back.'

According to a spokesperson for a music academy, the monthly cost for vocal, **choreography** and **composition** lessons is about one million won (US$840).

And what do teachers at such academies think of the prospects of these youngsters?

> **choreography:** designing and practising a dance sequence
>
> **composition:** song writing

'Hopeful singers must navigate a rocky path, because they have to stand the test of time despite the low probability of passing an audition,' says Noh Young-joo, president and CEO of music academy Power Vocal. 'I cannot give the exact figure, but the probability [of success] is extremely low. The hopefuls should create their own style of music and be **diligent** to increase their chances.'

What about criticism that K-pop idols are now being **churned out** of training academies just like products?

'Some agencies want their stars to follow their strategies and ideas, while others prefer having more individualistic artists,' Noh says. 'So aspiring singers have to analyse themselves first and decide which style they prefer. I do not think this is a matter of what is good and what is bad.'

> " Many agencies have been looking for foreign talent to target international markets. For instance, if a group has a Chinese member, it will be easier to set their sights on the Chinese market. "
>
> Noh Young-joo, president and CEO, Power Vocal

diligent: conscientious and hardworking

churned out: produced quickly without much care

1   The text you just read is about a young man following his dream, like the extract from *The Boy Who Harnessed the Wind* in Session 5.3.

Make some notes comparing Jeon Sung-won's story with William Kamkwamba's. Consider:

- the personal qualities of the two young men

- the attitude of others towards their work

- the differences in their success.

2   The article is from an online newspaper with a broad audience of adult readers. Articles like this often use a range of structural features to appeal to an audience looking for a quick, entertaining account of popular culture.

Write a paragraph evaluating the impact of the following features on the audience:

- the headline and bullet points

- the **pull quote** in the middle of the article

- the direct quotation from Jeon Sung-won

- the introduction of Noh Young-joo in the second part of the article.

> **Key words**
>
> **pull quote:** a quotation from an article that is highlighted as a graphic feature

3   'Reading between the lines' means working out meanings that are not explicitly stated in a text. On the surface, the K-pop article gives a straightforward account of Sung-won's experiences in the world of entertainment. However, the text contains other layers of meaning.

In small groups, discuss the following questions:

a   Does the article present Sung-won as heroic or foolish – or neither?

b   How is Young-joo presented – does he seem fair or is he taking advantage of people's dreams?

c   Is the article critical of K-pop?

Remember to explore areas of agreement and disagreement, and think carefully about your contributions to the discussion.

4   Write a personal response to the article, describing how you react to Sung-won's experiences in the world of entertainment. Using quotations, explain whether you have sympathy for him.

> **Writing tip**
>
> In some analytical writing, it is common to avoid writing in the first person ('I') as this helps to suggest a 'distance' and objectivity. In personal responses, however, using the first-person **perspective** can help to create a sense of sincerity and individual viewpoint.

> **Key word**
>
> perspective: the 'angle' that a story or account is told from – whose 'eyes' the reader sees it through

5 Your own beliefs and attitudes towards music and entertainment will have influenced your response to the previous activity. For example, if you enjoy K-pop music, then you may have found the article interesting and viewed Sung-won with some admiration or sympathy. If you are unfamiliar with K-pop, or you do not like the genre, you may have responded negatively.

Write a paragraph explaining what influenced your reaction to the article.

- How easy was it to analyse the way your views and prejudices affected your view?
- Do you think that beliefs and attitudes are helpful or not?

Summary checklist

- [ ] I can compare the features of two texts that have a similar focus.
- [ ] I can understand and explain the impact of organisational features in an article.
- [ ] I can contribute to an effective discussion about responses to a text.
- [ ] I can analyse how my own context influences my reactions to a text and its themes.

> 5.5 Animals and entertainment

In this session, you will:

- discuss your reaction to a persuasive text
- consider the effect of political language in an article
- explore how different contexts affect interpretations of a text
- consider your own context and analyse its effect on your response to a text.

Getting started

In pairs, discuss a time when a friend tried to persuade you to do something. How did they do it? Can you recall any particular words and phrases they used? Did you do what they wanted in the end? Why or why not?

Animals for entertainment?

The online article below intends to persuade readers that animals should not be used for entertainment purposes.

| Article | About | Home | 🔍 |

WHY WE SHOULDN'T USE ANIMALS FOR ENTERTAINMENT

Why do humans use animals for entertainment?

Why do humans enjoy **wielding their power** over animals?

Why do humans mistreat, cage, restrain animals and steal them from their natural **habitat**?

Why do humans enjoy making animals **submissive** by putting them in zoos and aquariums?

Let me tell you the facts.

> **wielding their power:** using power in a dominant way
>
> **habitat:** natural home
>
> **submissive:** accepting of being controlled

1 Confinement means prison

In a zoo, animals cannot explore or play naturally. They get less exercise, they can't interact with other animals and they become depressed. After years in confinement, their spirit is crushed and their behaviour is not normal. Animals are harmed physically and mentally by this cruel form of imprisonment.

2 A cage is not conservation

Zoos tell you that they are there to protect animals and help them. But if that's the case, why display animals for humans to stare at? Zoos are interested in money, not conservation. Cages are made for the entertainment of people, not to help animals.

conservation: protection

3 A sea park is no substitute for the ocean

No sight is more depressing than dolphins being forced to perform cheap tricks for the benefit of paying humans. Dolphins are bright, sociable, beautiful animals. Training and forcing them to entertain belittles their personalities. Keeping them in small aquariums is cruel and unnecessary. They belong in the ocean.

belittles: makes unimportant

4 Isolation is terrible

How would you like to be separated from other humans? If you've ever spent a long time on your own, you will know how lonely it is. So why take animals away from their own species? Separating family groups is unnatural.

5 Animals are not movie stars

A film set is not a natural place for a tiger, or any other animal. Who knows how many animals have been harmed or even killed when things go wrong? Are they cared for? I doubt it.

Next time you think about visiting a zoo, think again.

Next time you think about riding on the back of an animal, think again.

Next time you watch a film where animals have been forced to perform, think again.

Animals have feelings too.

They're not for your entertainment.

1   In pairs, discuss your reactions to the text.

    a   Do you agree with the views presented? Why or why not?

    b   What points could be made in a **counter-argument** to the article?

2   Persuasive texts often use political language. Politics is concerned with power, so political texts and language are about either challenging power or trying to keep hold of it. The article attempts to challenge the way people view animals, so it uses words and phrases designed to persuade readers to change their beliefs.

Features of political and persuasive texts include:

- emotive language

- presenting contrasting things as strongly positive or negative

- assertion (where views are stated without factual detail)

- presenting a biased rather than a balanced view.

Make brief notes on any examples of these features you can find in the article. Then, using relevant quotations, write a summary of the political language and how it influences your reaction.

3   Choose one paragraph from the article and write some sentences of your own that extend the view expressed in that paragraph. Try to match the voice of the article, and choose words and phrases that deliberately attempt to influence the reader's response.

> **Peer assessment**
>
> Swap work with a partner and give each other feedback.
>
> - How effective are their word choices? What impact will they have on the reader?
>
> - How closely have they matched the voice of the original text?

4   The 'context of production' is the background to a piece of writing – how, when and why it was written. To understand this type of context, you need to know where the text was originally published, who the intended readers were and the values of the culture to which the writer belonged.

Key word

counter-argument: an argument that presents an opposing viewpoint

Reading tip

One way to analyse the effect of emotive language is to consider possible replacement words. For example, replacing the emotive word 'slashed' with the word 'cut' should help you identify how the original word is intended to influence your reaction.

Here is some information about the context of the article:

- It is from a website about vegetarianism, which contains many articles about the treatment of animals.

- The article is unattributed – there is no writer's name attached to it.

- The original audience was people who are vegetarians, but a link to the article would have been shared on social media, bringing it to a wider audience.

- The article was written in 2005. At that time, many people visited zoos and less than 5 percent of the world's population were vegetarian.

In pairs, discuss how this contextual information helps you understand the writer's motivation for writing and their language choices.

5   The 'context of reception' refers to when, where and how the text is 'received' or read. When considering this context, think about what the attitudes and opinions of the reader might be, and what cultural or social values they might apply to their interpretation of the text.

In pairs, discuss how the following readers might respond to the article.

a   Jen read the article when a friend sent her a link to it. Jen is a vegetarian and animal lover, but most of the people in her country do not share her views.

b   Indra lives in a country where many people are vegetarian, including himself. He read the article for the first time when he saw it in this book. He has visited zoos.

c   Helmut first read the article in 2005, and he did not really agree with it. He is now an adult and regularly takes his young children to the local zoo.

6   Think back to your initial response to the article. Write a paragraph explaining how your own context affected your reaction. Consider:

- your own attitude and that of the culture in which you live towards zoos and animals generally

- your general response to persuasive articles and the style of this one in particular.

Summary checklist

☐ I can express a personal response to a persuasive text.

☐ I can identify political language in a text and explain its effects.

☐ I understand how different types of context affect interpretations of a text.

☐ I can explain my own context and how it influences my response to a text.

> 5.6 The benefits of zoos

In this session, you will:

- discuss an opinion article, considering its context

- compare the arguments made in two related texts

- explore the effect of language, punctuation and grammar choices

- write a balanced discursive response.

Getting started

Make a list of the most important skills and rules for group debate. Share your ideas with the class. Add to your list if there are suggestions you have not included that you think are useful.

'Why zoos are good'

The following article argues that zoos are good for animals. Before reading it, here are two pieces of contextual information:

- The article was published as an **opinion article** in *The Guardian*, a respected and popular UK newspaper.

- The writer, Dave Hone, tells the reader 'I am a lifelong fan of good zoos and have spent a number of years working as a volunteer keeper at two zoos so it is probably fair to say I'm firmly in the pro-zoo camp.'

Key words

opinion article: an article that gives one view on a topic, usually from an expert

1 In pairs, discuss how knowing these pieces of information before you read the article might influence your attitude and reaction towards it.

WHY ZOOS ARE GOOD

For many species (but no, not all) it is perfectly possible to keep them in a zoo or wildlife park and for them to have a quality of life as high or higher than in the wild. Their movement might be restricted (but not necessarily by that much) but they will not suffer from the threat or stress of **predators**, they won't suffer starvation and will get a varied and high-quality diet. A lot of very nasty things happen to truly 'wild' animals that simply don't happen in good zoos.

But what do zoos actually bring for the visitors and the wider world?

Conservation: Zoos protect against a species going **extinct**. A species protected in captivity can be bred up to provide foundation populations. A good number of species only exist in captivity and still more only exist in the wild because they have been reintroduced from zoos. Quite simply without these efforts there would be fewer species alive today and the world as a whole would be poorer for it.

Education: Many children and adults, especially those in cities, will never see a wild animal beyond a fox or pigeon, let alone a lion or giraffe. Sure television documentaries get ever more detailed and impressive, but that really does pale next to seeing a living creature in the flesh, hearing it, smelling it, watching what it does and having the time to absorb details. That alone will hopefully give them a greater appreciation for wildlife.

Research: If we are to save many wild species we need to know about how key species live, act and react. Being able to study animals in zoos where there is less risk means real changes can be effected on wild populations with far fewer problems. This can make a real difference to conservation efforts, providing knowledge for helping with the increasing threats of habitat destruction.

All in all with the ongoing global threats to the environment it's hard for me to see zoos as anything other than being essential to the long-term survival of numerous species. Sure there is always scope for improvement, but I think there can be few serious objections to good zoos. Without them, the world would be a much poorer place.

> **predator:** an animal that preys on others
> **extinct:** no longer in existence

2   In pairs, compare the arguments made about zoos in this article and the article in Session 5.5. Discuss:

- which of the two articles you find most convincing and why

- whether you think one or both articles are biased and why.

> ### Reading tip
>
> Remember that bias can be subtle. You will need to carefully consider the way facts are used and presented, and how fairly a text presents a view.

3   Write a 150-word analysis of how language, punctuation and grammar are used in the article on the previous page. Give examples of the following features, and comment on their overall effect – what impression do they create of the writer?

- **parentheses** and the comments within them in the first paragraph

- negative and positive language

- the pronouns 'we' and 'I'

- **adverbs of degree** and **adverbs of manner**, such as 'only' and 'simply'.

4   Using the information from this session and Session 5.5, plus your own knowledge and research, hold a group debate on the issue of zoos. Use appropriate language to suit the complexity of the topic. Discuss the possible benefits and disadvantages of zoos, taking notes as you go. Begin by deciding on roles within your group to suit your expertise.

5   You are going to write a **discursive response** to the topic of zoos. A discursive response gives an **objective** account of a variety of views about a topic. It usually:

- opens with an overview of the topic and a summary of the range of views that will be covered

- contains several paragraphs considering both the benefits and disadvantages of different views

- offers a conclusion that sums up the writer's view on the topic.

Write 300 words in formal, standard English. Use appropriate spelling strategies to ensure your writing is accurate.

Key words

parentheses: punctuation marks such as brackets, which enclose extra information

adverb of degree: an adverb that expresses the extent to which something is done (e.g. 'very', 'only', 'almost')

adverb of manner: an adverb expressing the way in which something is done (e.g. 'completely', 'simply', 'terribly')

discursive response: a piece of writing that discusses and explores different views

objective: not influenced by personal feelings

Writing tip

In a discursive response, the conclusion should give your personal view, but it should be written in formal language and avoid emotional content.

Summary checklist

- [ ] I can read and discuss an opinion article, including contextual information.
- [ ] I can compare the arguments made in two different texts on a similar topic.
- [ ] I can identify and analyse the effect of language, punctuation and grammar choices.
- [ ] I can write a discursive response, using a range of information and viewpoints.

Check your progress

Answer the following questions.

1 Summarise the features of the genre of comedy.

2 Explain, with examples, how contrast can be used as a device to create humour.

3 'Autobiography seems "real" and less crafted, but this is not really the case – autobiography is a shaped account.' Explain in your own words what this means, using examples.

4 Describe different types of organisational features found in newspaper and magazine articles and explain how they can help the intended readers.

5 Explain what political language is, including typical features.

6 Summarise what a discursive response is and how it is usually structured.

Project

In groups, you are going to plan the marketing campaign for a new musician. When a record company releases the music of a new star, lots of promotional material is required. This helps to market – publicise and 'sell' – the star to the public. The first decision concerns deciding how the star will be marketed – which TV shows, websites and audience will be targeted. Next, the following items are produced:

- written content for website and social media accounts

- a press release (a text given to news outlets) summarising background and music style

- the text of an interview with the star

- ideas and storyboards for music videos.

Your task is first of all to 'design' your music star. Decide 'their name', what type of music they perform, their general appearance (you could make some sketches) and the type of audience they will appeal to. You can also think of some song titles and maybe some lyrics too.

Divide up the various promotional tasks according to your expertise then set about writing the material. When finished, have a launch presentation where you explain your marketing campaign to the class and display your materials. Make sure each group member contributes to the presentation as confidently as possible. Use visual aids and notes as you feel appropriate.

After the presentations, hold a class vote for the best marketing campaign.

6 > A sense of place

In this unit, you will study a range of texts in which setting is a central feature. You will explore how a city is presented in fiction, study a piece of travel writing and a story featuring the same dramatic natural setting, and analyse a pair of poems about distinctive places.

> 6.1 The city sings

In this session, you will:

- read and perform a descriptive text
- explore the effect of language and structural choices in descriptive fiction
- write a response to a descriptive text
- create a vivid description of your own.

Getting started

In pairs, suggest ways that you could capture in writing the following noises. How would you write down and spell these sounds?

- the sound of a speeding car braking
- glass being smashed
- somebody running in boots
- a train rushing past.

If Nobody Speaks of Remarkable Things

The following extract is the opening of a novel by Jon McGregor.
It describes the sounds of a city.

1   Read the text aloud in pairs as accurately and confidently as you
    can. Take turns reading a paragraph each. The person who is not
    reading should try to make the sounds being described.

If you listen, you can hear it.

The city, it sings.

If you stand quietly, at the foot of a garden, in the middle of a street, on the roof of a house.

It's clearest at night, when the sound cuts more sharply across the surface of things, when the song reaches out to a place inside you.

It's a wordless song, for the most, but it's a song all the same, and nobody hearing it could doubt what it sings.

And the song sings the loudest when you pick out each note.

The low soothing hum of air-conditioners, fanning out the heat and the smells of shops and cafes and offices across the city, winding up and winding down, long breaths layered upon each other, a **lullaby** hum for tired streets.

The rush of traffic, even in the dark hours a constant crush of sound, tyres rolling and engines rumbling, loose drains clack-clacking like **castanets**.

Road-menders mending, choosing the hours of least interruption, **rupturing** the cold night air with drills, sweating beneath the fizzing hiss of floodlights, shouting to each other like drummers in rock bands calling out rhythms.

lullaby: a gentle song to help children to sleep

castanets: small pieces of wood clicked together to make a sound, usually to accompany Spanish dancing

rupturing: breaking or bursting

Lorries reversing, it seems every lorry in town is reversing, backing through gate-ways, easing up ramps, forklift trucks heaping and stacking and loading.

And all the alarms, calling for help, each street and estate, each every way you turn has alarms going off, coming on, going off, coming on, crying their needs to the night like babies waawaa-ing.

Sung sirens, sliding through the streets, through the darkest of the dark hours, a **lament** lifted high, held above the rooftops and fading away, lifted high, flashing past, fading away.

> lament: a sad piece of music

And all these things sing constant, the machines and the sirens, the cars, the hoots and the shouts and the hums and the crackles, all come together like a choir, sinking and rising with the turn of the wind, expecting more voices.

So listen.

Listen, and there is more to hear.

2   As you read the extract, you may have noticed the following grammatical and structural features:

   - Each paragraph contains a single sentence, with commas used to list things.

   - The extract begins and ends with simple sentences. Some of these use **imperatives** and address the reader directly.

In pairs, discuss the effect of these features and how they assist the writer's purpose.

> **Key word**
>
> imperative: a verb form used to give commands

3   The whole text is built around the metaphor of song – the noises of the city are compared to voices that come together 'like a choir'. Within this extended metaphor, the writer uses simile to describe some sounds.

Write about 100 words analysing the following similes, precisely identifying the effect and meanings created:

a   *loose drains clack-clacking like castanets*

b   *And all the alarms . . . crying their needs to the night like babies waawaa-ing.*

4   The overall effect of a text depends on several things, including the content, language choices and structural devices. Consider your own reaction to this extract, and write a response to the following task.

> **To what extent does *If Nobody Speaks of Remarkable Things* present the city as a threatening place? In your answer, you should comment on**:
>
> • your overall impression of the city
>
> • how the writer has used language and structural choices to present the city.

Select the most useful quotations and examples to support your points. Write about 250 words.

When analysing figurative language, remember to fully explore the different connotations of the comparison. One way to begin is to make a list of all of the associations of the comparison, especially positive and negative things.

Writing tip

When faced with 'to what extent' questions, remember that you are free to agree or disagree entirely (or partially) with the idea given in the question. There are no right or wrong views – a good response is demonstrated by the quality and strength of your argument.

5   Write a paragraph of up to 50 words in the style of *If Nobody Speaks of Remarkable Things*. Remember that the style is almost like poetry. Use some of the same features:

• aural and visual images

• comparisons

• long sentences with commas for listing

• **alliteration**

• verbs suggesting movement

• well-chosen adjectives.

Use one of the ideas in the Getting started activity or another image of your own.

Key word

alliteration: use of the same sound, especially consonants, at the beginning of several close-together words

Peer assessment

Swap books with another learner and read each other's paragraph aloud. Give your partner feedback on their writing. Comment on:

- which parts of the paragraph were most effective in creating the image of the city
- any suggested word changes that you think would improve the paragraph.

Summary checklist

☐ I can read, discuss and create sound effects for a distinctive city description.

☐ I can analyse the effect of language and structural choices in a description.

☐ I can write a response to a text, commenting on the effect of language and expressing my own reaction.

☐ I can use language, structure and grammatical features to create a short but vivid description.

> 6.2 A love letter to the Grand Canyon

In this session, you will:

- read and discuss the structure of a piece of travel writing
- explore meanings in two pieces of travel writing
- consider how humans' relationship with nature is presented in literature
- write your own descriptive text.

Getting started

In pairs, discuss places that are special to you – they can be in your local area, or places you have visited that left a lasting impression. Describe them to each other and explain the feelings they generate in you.

A love letter to the Grand Canyon

Read the following non-fiction text. It is a piece of travel writing by James Kaiser about the Grand Canyon – a huge valley in Arizona, USA.

I still remember the first time I walked to the edge of Grand Canyon. With each step the canyon yawned open wider, revealing **cascading** rock layers stretching across the horizon. I took a deep breath and tried to comprehend the scenery. It was 1996, I was 19 years old, and, having grown up in Maine, there was only one thing I could compare it to: the ocean. All that space, all those natural patterns. But unlike the ocean, Grand Canyon seemed frozen in time.

After spending a few minutes, I pulled out a camera, snapped a few shots, and headed to Las Vegas. Ever since Spanish explorers set eyes on Grand Canyon, people have struggled to understand what, exactly, they are looking at. Some things – the best things – require more than an afternoon to fully appreciate.

Nearly a decade later, I returned to Grand Canyon. I spent months exploring, seeking out stunning viewpoints and observing how the light changed hour-to-hour, day-to-day, season-to-season.

One morning I watched the sun rise after a winter snowstorm. Clouds swirled through the canyon while a soft blanket of snow melted to feed spring wildflowers. The wildflowers **wilted** under a blazing summer sun. And the summer sun kicked up thunderstorms that lasted until autumn.

Grand Canyon is not, I realized, a **static** place.

Viewed over millions of years, towering rock formations melt away like ice sculptures. Cliffs crumble like dice.

The more I learned, the more I wanted to explore the depths of Grand Canyon. That opportunity came. Drifting deep into the heart of Grand Canyon, we descended through time. We reached Vishnu Schist, a **gnarled** black rock nearly half the age of Earth. Floating through narrow corridors of Vishnu Schist was **humbling** – a rare glimpse into our planet's distant past.

Much remained mysterious, but Grand Canyon was slowly coming into focus.

Note: this text uses American spellings.

cascading: moving or hanging downwards

wilted: became limp

static: lacking in movement or change

gnarled: rough and twisted with age

humbling: being made to feel less important

1   Using the most appropriate reading strategy, locate and write down some quotations that show the different responses the writer has towards the Canyon at different points in his life.

2   The writer structures the text by including a reference to his earlier visit to the Canyon as a 19-year-old, and contrasting this with his later visit and the feelings it brings.

Using your notes from Activity 1, write a paragraph explaining the effect of this structural choice. What does it imply about the writer and the Canyon's effect upon him?

3   In Sessions 1.5 and 1.6 you studied an article about Coober Pedy. You saw how travel writing often ends with the writer showing or implying what they have learnt from their travels. Here are some of the big ideas you considered in relation to the writer's experience of Coober Pedy:

- there are many different ways of living, and they are all equal

- humans have the same feelings and ambitions wherever they live

- modern living is destroying old ways of living.

In small groups, discuss the big ideas in 'A love letter to the Grand Canyon'. What differences and/or similarities do you notice in the ideas here and those in the article on Coober Pedy? Explore these complex ideas in detail using appropriate language.

Reading tip

Remember that terms like 'big ideas', 'themes' and 'significance' are often used interchangeably in English studies. They all are concerned with the concepts of the texts – the meanings that you see in a piece of writing, and the main points the writer is exploring.

Nature, and the way humans interact with it, is a significant theme in literature. For example, **Romantic literature** presents nature as a force that inspires humans. Its scale and beauty seem immense next to humans. In this type of writing, nature causes people to feel a kind of awe, a mixture of wonder and fear, which is known as 'the sublime'. You can see a representation of this idea in the picture on the previous page – the man seems very small compared to the vast, impressive landscape around him.

4   Although 'A love letter to the Grand Canyon' is a modern piece of travel writing, the writer echoes the genre of Romantic literature.

   In pairs:

   a   Identify lines from the text that show the writer's feelings about nature.

   b   Summarise what the writer 'learns' from nature – how does it change his understanding about life?

5   Write your own paragraph about the wonder of the natural world. Choose language carefully to create a sense of the scale and beauty of the landscape you are describing. Focus on the visual imagery of the scenery and the feelings it creates. (Paragraph 7 from 'A love letter to the Grand Canyon' is a good example to follow.)

   You could base your description on one of the photographs in this session or choose your own place to describe. Before you start, decide how much planning (if any) you need to do for this task.

> ### Key words
>
> **Romantic literature:** a genre of writing from the 18th and 19th centuries, which focuses on ideas about emotion, imagination and nature

> ### Writing tip
>
> Figurative language can help to portray scenery vividly in descriptive writing. Experiment with techniques such as personification, which can help to convey a sense of life and movement.

Summary checklist

- [ ] I can comment on the structure of a piece of travel writing.
- [ ] I can compare and contrast meaning and ideas in two pieces of travel writing.
- [ ] I can analyse how humans' relationship with nature is presented in literature.
- [ ] I can use language and structural techniques to write a vivid description of nature.

> 6.3 Chasm

In this session, you will:

- predict the plot of a story from its title
- explore the dialogue in a story with a metaphorical setting
- consider the effect of using a focal character
- explore the meaning of a spatial metaphor.

Getting started

Most stories feature characters that readers like or sympathise with. In pairs, discuss stories featuring characters that you do *not* like. Why do you feel that way? How does the writer make these characters unsympathetic?

'Chasm'

The extract on the next page is from a short story called 'Chasm'. It is set in Milford Sound, a national park in New Zealand. It features Adrian and Janice, who are father and grown-up daughter. They haven't been close in the past, but now that they are older, Adrian is hoping that he and his daughter might be able to develop a better relationship. They agree to visit a famous chasm (a deep crack in the earth's surface) as part of a day out.

1   Before you read the extract, note down any thoughts you have about the title. What does it lead you to expect in the story? The literal and metaphorical definitions of 'chasm' are:

- a very deep hole that seems to have no bottom
- a very bad situation that will not improve
- a unbridgeable gap between two things or people.

Reading tip

Writers choose their titles carefully, so always consider the significance of a title before *and* after you read a story or extract. Consider whether the title takes on extra significance once you know what happens.

44

Surrounded by damp trees on all sides, it was difficult to know how far away the chasm was. There seemed to be a queue of people up ahead dressed in bright-coloured coats. Their **murmuring** voices seemed to suggest excitement, but the sound of gushing water from the nearby waterfall drowned out the detail of their words.

After a few moments shuffling through the trees, Adrian found himself on a bridge over the chasm. They were finally there, surrounded by happy parents taking pictures of their children **squealing** in delight, and the open sky. He found it a bit disappointing, if he was honest. He looked at his daughter, watching **flecks** of moisture and sunlight on her face. The drive here had been a little tense. He opened his mouth, but Janice spoke first.

'We don't need words,' she said, looking down into the chasm beneath them.

She was enjoying this, he thought, but he couldn't really see why. It certainly wasn't peaceful, given the crowds. It wasn't nice to look at either. Just some brown rocks far below them and empty, damp air. He couldn't really see why they had come here. A three-hour drive to look at . . . well, brown rocks.

'What do you feel, dad?' asked Janice after a while, her eyes searching her father's face.

'Nothing,' he said. Even as the word came out, he knew he shouldn't have said it.

'Nothing?' she said, annoyed. 'One of nature's most **profound** places and you feel nothing? Can't you feel the years of history? Doesn't it move you?'

Around them, some of the tourists were shifting uncomfortably, aware of the note of tension.

'We could have gone for lunch somewhere instead,' he said. 'Perhaps we still can.'

Janice looked at him, saying nothing, but remembering the years of **dispute** between them.

'Well, then how does it make you feel?' he asked her, finally.

'Alive,' she said. 'It makes me feel at peace, and it makes me sad.'

'Why sad?'

'Do you even need to ask?' she said quietly.

---

murmuring: a low, continuous sound

squealing: a high-pitched cry
flecks: small specks of something

profound: intense or deep
dispute: conflict or disagreement

2 In pairs, explore the dialogue between Adrian and Janice.

   a Discuss what the dialogue suggests about the two characters' emotions.

   b Read the dialogue aloud using your voices dramatically and confidently to express the range of emotions shown.

- How does reading aloud and using drama approaches help your learning?
- Do you find it useful? Why or why not?

3 Although 'Chasm' is told in the **third person**, Adrian is used as the **focal character**. This means that the audience is shown more of his view than any other character's. There is evidence for this in paragraph 2, which includes the phrase *he found it a bit disappointing*, and gives an account of Adrian's thoughts. Notice how this invites the reader to 'see' Janice through his eyes.

In pairs, discuss the effect of this structural choice. When you have finished exploring a range of ideas, give your own personal response to the characters. Below are some statements to prompt your discussion. How far do you agree with them?

- Readers see Adrian as a sympathetic character – because of the way the story is told, they feel a little sorry for him.

- The way the story is told makes readers feel sorry for Janice – they can see why Adrian annoys her.

- Readers find both characters unsympathetic.

4 In this story, the setting acts as a **spatial metaphor** for the characters' relationship. The chasm comes to represent the 'distance' between Adrian and Janice.

Write a 100-word analysis of the different reactions Adrian and Janice have to the chasm. Using appropriate references from the text, comment on:

- their feelings and attitudes to the chasm

- the spatial metaphor and what it implies about their relationship.

Reading tip

When analysing dialogue, always consider the context of the surrounding story. Think about what is happening and whether the dialogue explicitly shows these feelings, or whether it suggests that the characters are saying one thing but thinking another.

Key words

third person: written from an observer's point of view using pronouns such as 'he', 'she' and 'they'

focal character: the character that draws the reader's attention – sometimes, but not always, a main character or narrator

spatial metaphor: a metaphor that uses a space (i.e. a physical place, location or area) as a comparison

Summary checklist

- ☐ I understand the significance of a title and can predict possible plot ideas based on it.
- ☐ I can interpret a story with a metaphorical setting, including the dialogue.
- ☐ I can explain the effect of using a focal character in a story and give a personal response.
- ☐ I can analyse the different meanings of a spatial metaphor in a short story.

❯ 6.4 In the desert

In this session, you will:

- identify information and layers of meaning in a poem
- consider the effect of irony and contrast
- explore the conventions of a sonnet
- write an analysis of the significance of setting.

Getting started

Below is a list of things mentioned in the poem you are going to explore in this session. In pairs, use this information to discuss where the poem might be set and what it might be about:

- a huge pair of stone legs
- a stone face in the sand
- a bragging king
- a large desert.

'Ozymandias'

The poem 'Ozymandias' by Percy Bysshe Shelley features a desert setting. The narrator recounts meeting a traveller who describes finding a statue of Ozymandias in the desert. Ozymandias is the Greek name for the ancient Egyptian ruler Rameses II.

I met a traveller from an **antique** land,

Who said: 'Two vast and trunkless legs of stone

Stand in the desert. Near them, on the sand,

Half sunk, a shattered **visage** lies, whose frown,

And wrinkled lip, and **sneer** of cold command,

Tell that its sculptor well those passions read

Which yet survive, stamped on these lifeless things,

The hand that mocked them, and the heart that fed.

And on the **pedestal**, these words appear:

"My name is Ozymandias, king of kings:

Look on my works, ye mighty, and despair!"

Nothing beside remains. Round the decay

Of that **colossal** wreck, **boundless** and bare,

The lone and level sands stretch far away.'

antique: ancient
visage: face
sneer: a mocking smile
pedestal: the base of a statue
colossal: huge
boundless: never-ending

1   In pairs, read the poem and discuss:

 • the appearance of the statue and what it suggests about the passing of time

 • the way the sculptor (the person who made the statue) has presented Ozymandias's face and what this suggests about the ruler's personality

 • what the words on the pedestal tell you about the ruler's sense of self-importance.

2   When the statue that the traveller describes was first erected, it would have been surrounded by grand buildings and structures symbolising the pharaoh Rameses's power. Now, however, *nothing beside remains*.

Consider how the poem's setting links to its meaning. Write a paragraph explaining the **irony** that arises from the contrast of the bragging words on the pedestal and the description of the setting that the traveller gives.

Key word

irony: an effect showing a different or opposite outcome of what was intended

3   In Session 5.5 you explored how political language is concerned with power. 'Ozymandias' explores issues of power and time, so it has something to say about political ideas.

In pairs, discuss the following learners' descriptions of the poem. Find lines from the poem to support each interpretation.

A
The setting of the poem is really important. The poem is all about how time and nature are more powerful than humans. These elements have beaten the ruler – his statue is a wreck and its face is buried in the sand. The description of the desert is important, as it shows that we humans are less important than we think we are.

B
The poem criticises people who enjoy their power too much. Ozymandias seems arrogant and very pleased with his own power, but as the writer shows, his power doesn't last. I like how Ozymandias has just turned into a little story – a footnote in history – rather than the great man he thought he was. The final lines are key to showing this.

4   Ozymandias is written as a **sonnet**, a poetic form that has been used since the 13th century. Although there are some variations in the form, a sonnet usually follows these conventions:

- one stanza containing 14 lines

- lines written in **iambic pentameter**

- a regular rhyme scheme, usually ABAB CDCD EFEF GG, or ABBAABBA CDECDE

- the inclusion of a **volta**

- a **couplet** in the final lines.

In pairs, identify which of these conventions the poet has used in 'Ozymandias'. Where a convention has been omitted or adapted, try to comment on the effect this creates.

> **Key words**
>
> **sonnet:** a poetic form that consists of a single stanza of 14 lines
>
> **iambic pentameter:** a line of poetry containing ten syllables with five main beats in the line
>
> **volta:** a turning point or shift, for example where a new idea is introduced
>
> **couplet:** two successive lines of poetry (usually the same length) that rhyme

5 Sonnets are usually about love – either celebrating its joy or showing the heartache it causes. 'Ozymandias' is unusual in this respect, as its themes are power, nature and time.

Read the learners' ideas below about the reasons for and effect of these choices in the poem. Which ideas do you agree with and why?

A Although the subject matter is different to a usual sonnet, it is still about love in a way – the self-love of Ozymandias. It shows how self-interested he was, and like a tragic relationship, it ends badly for him.

B The poem is a sort of ironic sonnet – the poet is playing with conventions, and wants the reader to see this. Making the setting so prominent helps the poem seem more like a story than a poem.

6 Write a 250-word analysis of the significance of setting in 'Ozymandias'. Use the key words to help you analyse language and structure. Comment on:

- how the setting contributes to the ideas in the poem
- the contrast between the setting and the words of the ruler
- the way language and structural choices are used to convey the setting.

Writing tip

Responses about the 'significance' of something require you to focus on meanings and ideas, so make sure these points are central to your response. Comments on language and structure should be given to support these points.

Summary checklist

- [ ] I can identify information and explore layers of meaning in a poem.
- [ ] I can comment on irony and contrast and the effect these have in a poem.
- [ ] I understand the conventions of a sonnet, including structure and theme.
- [ ] I can analyse the significance of setting in a poem, considering language and structural choices.

> ## 6.5 Pastoral poetry

In this session, you will:

- explore the structure and language of a modern sonnet
- learn about the conventions of pastoral literature
- use poetic structures for effect
- compare the use of couplets in two related texts.

Getting started

In pairs, discuss how the countryside is represented in books you have read. What qualities and atmospheres are created in texts featuring rural settings?

'Vermont'

You are going to read another sonnet: 'Vermont' by Phillip Whidden. The place setting is an area known as New England in the USA. This is central to the poem, but the time setting is important too. Autumn is a time of change, but it is also a very pretty season in this part of the world.

A white wood house defines the slope. The trees
Have gone to red and flame. A field beyond
Is spread with grass and **granite** rocks at ease.
This **stonewall pattern** thinks it holds a pond,
But it is free beneath October's sun,
At least as free as anything can be
In fever such as we all know when, done
With heavy summer, eyes begin to see
The chill of air and glaze themselves with dreams
Restrained. The farmhouse windows have their fire
Inside as well. **Twilight** is more, it seems,
And **maple** facts can **mesmerize** desire.
   A white wood house defines the slope of hill
     Where people keep another autumn, still.

granite: a very hard rock

stonewall pattern: the arrangement of stone

twilight: the period between daylight and darkness

maple: a tree with colourful autumn leaves

mesmerize: capture the attention; hypnotise

1 Make notes in answer to these questions.

   a Describe the sonnet form used in the poem. Comment on rhyme scheme and use of iambic pentameter.

   b Summarise the overall impression of Vermont you get from the poem. Refer to the visual, aural and tactile images in the poem.

Pastoral literature is a genre that features countryside settings, usually in an idealised way (in a very positive manner). The text below explains some features of pastoral literature.

> In pastoral literature, the countryside is celebrated: it is shown to be a place of beauty and peace. The real countryside obviously contains negative things such as death and hardship, but pastoral literature mainly gives readers a **sentimental** version of the countryside. It is a place where humans and nature are in harmony. Where human-made structures such as houses are shown, they sit peacefully alongside nature rather than spoiling it. In pastoral texts, nature is never threatening – often, humans are inspired by and learn from nature. There is also a sense of **nostalgia**, as if writers are looking back to happier, more carefree times. In some examples of the genre, there is a hint that change is coming, as if the good times cannot last forever.

> **Key words**
>
> **pastoral literature:** texts featuring countryside settings

> **sentimental:** an exaggerated feeling of tenderness or sadness
>
> **nostalgia:** an affection or longing for the past

2 In pairs, find the features of pastoral literature mentioned in the text above in the sonnet 'Vermont'. List quotations that match the features.

3 The arrangement of lines in poetry, along with other structural features such as **enjambment** and **caesura**, can support the meaning of the poem. For example, in lines 9 and 10 of 'Vermont', the poet writes:

The chill of air and glaze themselves with dreams / Restrained.

Here, the rhythm of the first line has a pace – the iambic pentameter carries it onward, then the enjambment pushes the reader to the next line. The caesura in the next line comes after the word 'restrained'. The idea expressed in these lines is that summer has ended and that dreams are restrained. The caesura reinforces this idea, as if the summer comes to a full stop.

> **Key words**
>
> **enjambment:** where one sentence of poetry continues on to the line below
>
> **caesura:** a break within a line of poetry where either punctuation or the rhythm of the poem indicates a pause

Write two lines of pastoral poetry in a similar style. Use iambic pentameter, and experiment with enjambment and caesura. Write about:

- the leaves starting to fall from the trees

- the sun going down at the end of the day.

Writing a line of poetry in iambic pentameter is a trial-and-error process – it can be like solving a puzzle. Start by getting the basic idea for the line, then rearrange and replace words until the rhythm fits.

Peer assessment

Take turns to read each other's lines aloud. Feed back to your partner, commenting on the following.

- The accuracy of the iambic pentameter – does it follow the pattern?

- The use of enjambment and caesura – does it create a useful effect?

Language focus

A couplet is a common feature of poetry and dialogue in some plays. Couplets tend to rhyme and are usually placed at the end of a poem or scene. Couplets often – but not always – give a sense of 'completion', as if something is being summed up or concluded. They can be used for different effects in writing.

Here is the final couplet from a sonnet in which the narrator says that despite the length of her marriage, she is still loved:

- We were married very long ago,

  But you still love me and you tell me so.

The rhyme and the lack of caesura contribute to the sense of completion – the happiness of the narrator is reflected in the 'perfection' of the way the lines are written.

Now consider another example. Here, an older parent reflects on how they feel now their child has left home:

- My child is grown and I am sad they've gone

  Away, now I must face life on my own.

In this example, there is less feeling of completion – the writer forces the word 'Away' onto the next line and the rhyme of 'gone' and 'own' is not exact. This couplet feels much less 'perfect', reflecting the sad feelings of the narrator.

4   Read these final couplets from 'Ozymandias' and 'Vermont'.

> Of that colossal wreck, boundless and bare
> The lone and level sands stretch far away.

> A white wood house defines the slope of hill
>   Where people keep another autumn, still.

Compare how language and structural features are combined to present the ideas in these couplets. Comment on:

- word choices
- visual images
- iambic pentameter, rhyme and caesura.

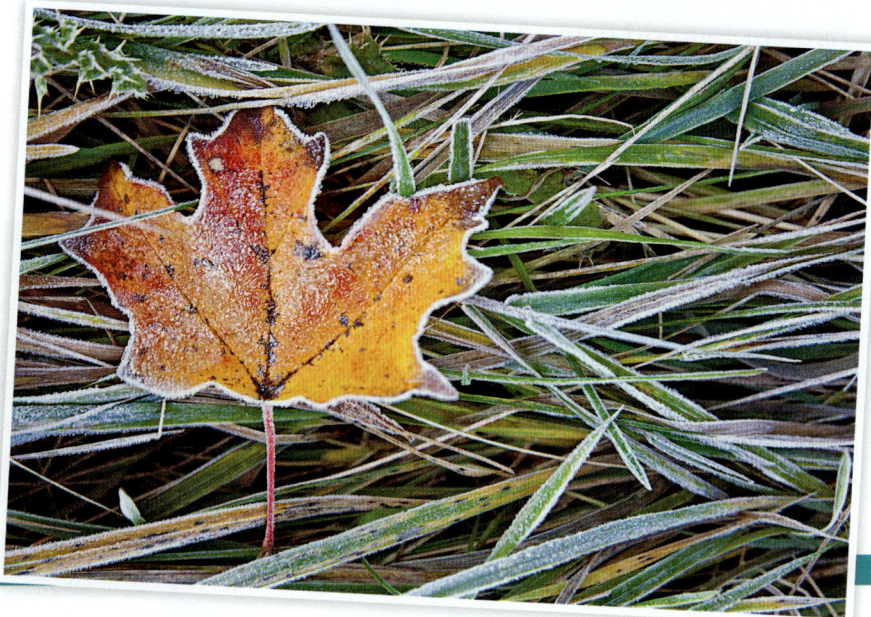

Summary checklist

- ☐ I can describe and analyse the effects of structure and language in a modern sonnet.
- ☐ I understand and can identify the conventions of pastoral literature.
- ☐ I can write some lines of poetry using structural features for effect.
- ☐ I can compare the way ideas are presented in couplets in two related texts.

> 6.6 Returning home

In this session, you will:

- respond to audio and written texts about returning home
- consider the effect of pathetic fallacy
- explore the effect of non-chronological features
- write a sentimental account.

Getting started

In pairs, discuss what you associate with the word 'home'. What connotations does the word have, and what ideas and feelings does it hold for you?

1 Listen to the audio recording, in which Martika talks about returning home. Make notes on her thoughts and feelings about this experience, then write an explanation of the effect the account has on you as a listener.

Tales from the Riverbank

The following extract is from the autobiography *Tales from the Riverbank*. Here, the writer describes a sentimental return to his home village of Paavola, Finland, after years of travelling abroad.

> The steering wheel of the hire car felt odd in my hands. Driving away from the airport, I realised I hadn't sat inside a car for three years, let alone driven one.
>
> Being back in Finland feels strange. The light is different here. And the place is full of memories.
>
> In some ways, it seemed only yesterday I said goodbye to my father and set off on my adventure; in some ways, it seemed like an age since I'd seen him.

Listening tip

Engaging with the thoughts and feelings of other speakers gives you the opportunity to experience different points of view. When listening to such accounts, focus on the emotions being expressed and try to understand where they come from and how you would feel in the same situation.

Communication has been difficult. It's hard to get a phone signal in a jungle in Borneo, and my dad isn't very **tech-savvy**. But he is, as men of his generation are, a keen letter writer.

And there were times when his letters really helped. He'd send them to various stopping-off points in capital cities and I'd collect them when I could. Once, after a **harrowing** journey through Sudan, I picked up his letter from a post office in Khartoum and stood on a street corner quietly reading his words. One line remained with me.

The leaves on the silver birch trees are beginning to turn yellow.

It said nothing and everything.

I've covered some miles in the last three years, but the journey home was longest of all. The roads felt **anonymous**, the miles longer than they should have been, and the concrete and metal so very different from my life abroad.

Yet nature has a way of **rejuvenating** humans and as I reached the outskirts of Paavola, the beauty of Finland's summer struck me. The natural light of the sky called me home and as I reached the top of the hill, the green valley below spread its arms in open welcome.

I parked the car. Walking up the narrow path to my father's cottage, I felt a sense of nervous excitement creep over me. The swallows were here, darting and swooping as they went about their nest-building. There were green leaves on the silver birches.

He was standing at the door.

'Welcome home, son,' he smiled.

tech-savvy: knowing a lot about modern technology

harrowing: very distressing

anonymous: nameless, unremarkable

rejuvenating: making someone feel younger or more energetic

2   In pairs, discuss the significance of the two references to silver birch trees.

Language focus

Pathetic fallacy is a type of figurative language where the writer uses the natural world to reflect the emotions of people in a story. For example, in pathetic fallacy, weather may embody a character's situation:

- Sidhra walked sadly along the path, her shoulders slumped. The never-ending rain soaked her to the skin.

Here, Sidhra's sadness is embodied by the rain, which is 'never-ending'. The implication is that Sidhra's sadness may also be long-lasting.

However, pathetic fallacy is more than the use of weather; it refers to anywhere that a character's emotions are projected onto an aspect of nature. Consider what is suggested here:

- Corin strode across the field, the wind blowing furiously through the long grass, whipping his legs. Up ahead was a large cliff, its rocky summit pointing aggressively to the sky.

Here, Corin's emotions are not stated explicitly in the text, they are transferred to nature. The reader understands that Corin is feeling fury and aggression.

An added effect of pathetic fallacy is that it invites the reader to anticipate what may happen later in the story. In the example above, we expect some type of conflict or confrontation to occur. This creates an element of tension.

Key words

pathetic fallacy: a figurative technique in which nature is used to reflect characters' emotions or situations

3   Write a detailed analysis of the use and effect of pathetic fallacy in *Tales from the Riverbank*. Using quotations from the last few paragraphs of the story, explain:

- how the scenery around Paavola reflects the narrator's feelings
- the impact these descriptions are likely to have upon the reader.

4   Although the writer's journey from the airport to home is told chronologically, it includes a brief flashback to his time in Sudan.

In pairs, discuss the effect of including the following elements of the story:

- the brief reference to his journey through Sudan
- the line from his father's letter.

5 Write your own imaginative account of returning home. Write 300 words in the voice of an older person, trying to create a sentimental feeling similar to that in *Tales from the Riverbank*.

Experiment with ways of structuring your writing, perhaps using flashbacks and pathetic fallacy. Remember to write in standard English and use appropriate strategies to spell complex words accurately.

Use one of these ideas, or choose one of your own:

- a person returning home after a long stay in hospital
- an elderly person returning to their childhood home overseas.

- How did you approach the planning and writing of this account?
- What were the challenges and how did you overcome them?

Summary checklist

- [ ] I can respond confidently to ideas in spoken and written texts.
- [ ] I understand the meaning and effects of pathetic fallacy.
- [ ] I can comment on the effect of non-chronological features in a piece of autobiographical writing.
- [ ] I can write an imaginative account in a particular voice, creating deliberate emotions and effects.

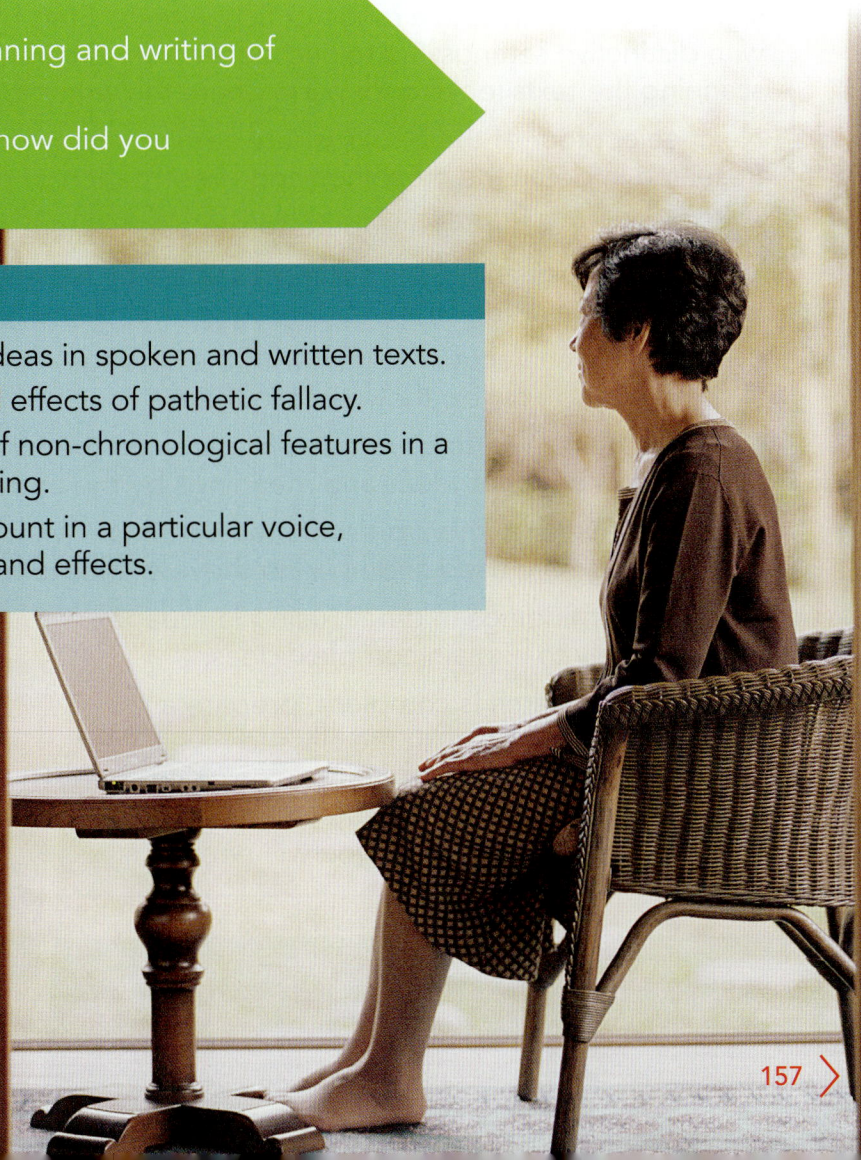

Check your progress

Answer the following questions.

1   Note down some tips for learners who want to write a vivid description of a setting.

2   Explain some of the typical ways that writers present the natural landscape, including the concept of the sublime.

3   Explain what a focal character is and what effects on the reader the use of a focal character can have in a story.

4   Write a summary of the conventions of a sonnet.

5   Describe the features of pastoral literature.

6   Using examples, explain what the term 'pathetic fallacy' means and the effects it can create.

Project

In this unit you have seen how places and settings can be much more than just a backdrop to a story. They can be central to the meaning of a text and may represent characters' feelings and show humans' bond with the landscape and home.

In groups of four, you are going to research and present a project about the significance of places in a range of fiction texts. Start by making a collection of books with distinctive settings. Try to find books from different genres. Spend some time scanning the texts looking for parts where the writer focuses on setting.

Next, select four of the books where setting seems particularly significant. Research in detail the meanings and presentation of place. You could look at:

- What the settings contribute to the atmosphere of the stories.

- What values and ideas are represented by the settings – for example, is there anything to be said about power, secrecy or freedom?

- How the characters interact with the settings – what is their relationship with them, and how do they react to them?

- Whether the settings remains 'static' – do they develop during the book, or take on different ideas and meanings by the end of the story?

- The way the authors presents the settings – what sort of techniques and language are used and how do they contribute to the overall impact?

Discuss your findings in detail, using language appropriately to explain complex ideas.

Once your research is complete, prepare a presentation to share with the class to reveal your findings. This could be an oral presentation, a display or an online document. You can decide what level of visual support you will need.

7 'The Journey Within'

In this unit you will study a short story called 'The Journey Within' by Annelise Heurtier. You will explore and write in the genre of fantasy, analyse structure and language features, and consider the meanings of the story.

> 7.1 The Tree

In this session, you will:

- identify explicit and deeper meanings in a story opening
- explore the implications of a motif
- write an account using features of the fantasy genre.

Getting started

In Session 4.4 you learnt about some features of the fantasy genre. Using this knowledge, the title of the story ('The Journey Within') and the titles of the six sessions in this unit, make some predictions in pairs about what might happen in the story.

The Tree   The farmers   The bronze door   The crow   Nothing   Chosen One

'The Journey Within'

Read the opening of 'The Journey Within'. Celegorn is Aveleen's father.

Extract 1

Aveleen kicked off her boots and let out a long sigh.

She had been walking for two days solid. How could it be that the Brown Mountain still seemed so far away? Had she taken a wrong turn and set off down one of those **devious**, false trails that send you round and round in circles?

Her body was slumped against the rock where she had stopped to rest. Her stomach churned with distress. Would she be back in time? Would she reward the trust that Celegorn had placed in her? Aveleen grabbed her **waterskin** and took three **anguished** gulps.

No matter how clear the signs, she still refused to accept that her father would soon be joining the Other Worlds. He may have been well past his 150th season, but he still seemed so . . . youthful. Not once had his body shown any sign of **fatigue**. Not once had his mind **flagged**.

Yet the Tree had spoken. And the Tree was never wrong. A handful of its leaves had started to turn silver, a clear sign that for Celegorn the end was **nigh**. The time had come to find a new Chosen One to lead the people for the next cycle.

Many hopefuls had appeared in turn before the Tree. Like Lothar, the engraver's eldest son, who was said to have battled a Giant. Or Amæthon and Govannon, both born leaders of men. And others still, all spurred on by their determination to rule.

Yet for the first time in her people's history, the Tree had rejected each and every candidate.

Who was the unwitting Chosen One? Her friend Olirin, who had departed six moons ago to explore the kingdoms of the North? But he was just a child, too young to deem himself a leader. Would she find the answer at the top of the Brown Mountain, as her father had assured her?

Deep in thought, Aveleen pulled on her dust-covered boots and returned the waterskin to her pack. If she was going to daydream, she may as well do it on the move, otherwise she would stand no

---

devious: deceptive, underhand

waterskin: a container for carrying water

anguished: experiencing pain or suffering

fatigue: extreme tiredness

flagged: become less energetic

nigh: near

chance of being back before the last leaf on the Tree turned stiff with silver.

She was in a very strange place: a vast plain dotted with rocks, ash trees and sea buckthorn. It resembled her own land, but at the same time it was different. Two suns shone in the white sky. The plants swayed despite the lack of any breeze. Where was she, exactly? She was not even sure if the region had a name.

1   Use an appropriate reading strategy to find and make notes on information in the text that shows details about:

- the purpose of Aveleen's journey

- her feelings about the journey

- what is happening to Celegorn

- the strange setting.

Write a paragraph explaining how these details help to create an interesting opening.

2   Fantasy stories combine magical elements with recognisable
    real-life ones.

    In pairs, reread the extract and identify magical and 'real' items,
    actions and concepts in the story. Discuss the overall effect of this
    combination – what does it add to the story and what effect does it
    have on the reader?

Language focus

A **motif** is a repeated idea or image in a text. It can be a phrase,
an action or a symbol that occurs in different parts of a story.
Motifs can help readers identify important themes in a text.
As a motif is repeated and developed, its meanings might be
extended. Look at this example of a how a wedding ring could
be used a motif:

- In the first chapter of a novel, a female character gets
  married. Her wedding ring is a sign of love, harmony and
  happiness. Later in the story, it becomes a source of sadness
  and a symbol of memories upon the death of her husband.
  In the final part of the story, the woman gives the ring to her
  daughter for her own marriage and it comes to represent
  themes of renewal and family history.

Key word

motif: a repeated
idea, image or
symbol in a text

---

3   The Tree is introduced in the opening part of the story, and it
    becomes a recurring motif. In pairs, explore how the motif is
    established in Extract 1. Discuss:

    - the Tree's power in the world of the story

    - the link between Celegorn and the Tree

    - the connotations of trees (what readers normally associate
      with them).

4   The writer includes brief details about other characters who have
    been rejected by the Tree, including *Lothar, the engraver's eldest
    son, who was said to have battled a Giant.*

    Write a short account of Lothar's meeting with the Tree.
    Use anything you have learnt from the extract, as well as your
    own imagination, to bring this scene to life.

- Decide how much planning you will need to do before you write.

- Write about 250 words in standard English.

- Use language appropriate to the fantasy genre, such as references to unusual aspects of setting, and descriptions of Lothar as a brave, distinctive character.

- Use appropriate language techniques.

- Experiment with different ways of structuring the account.

- How much planning did you decide to do?
- Did you feel you made the right decision? Why or why not?

Writing tip

When writing a scene between two characters, consider how much of the story you will tell through dialogue and how much the narrator will tell. Many stories start with the narrator's voice, but you could try experimenting with dialogue in the first line of your story.

Summary checklist

☐ I understand the implications of explicit information and can explore deeper layers of meaning in a story opening.
☐ I can understand and analyse the purpose and implications of a motif.
☐ I can choose an appropriate structure for a fictional account and write it using features of the fantasy genre.

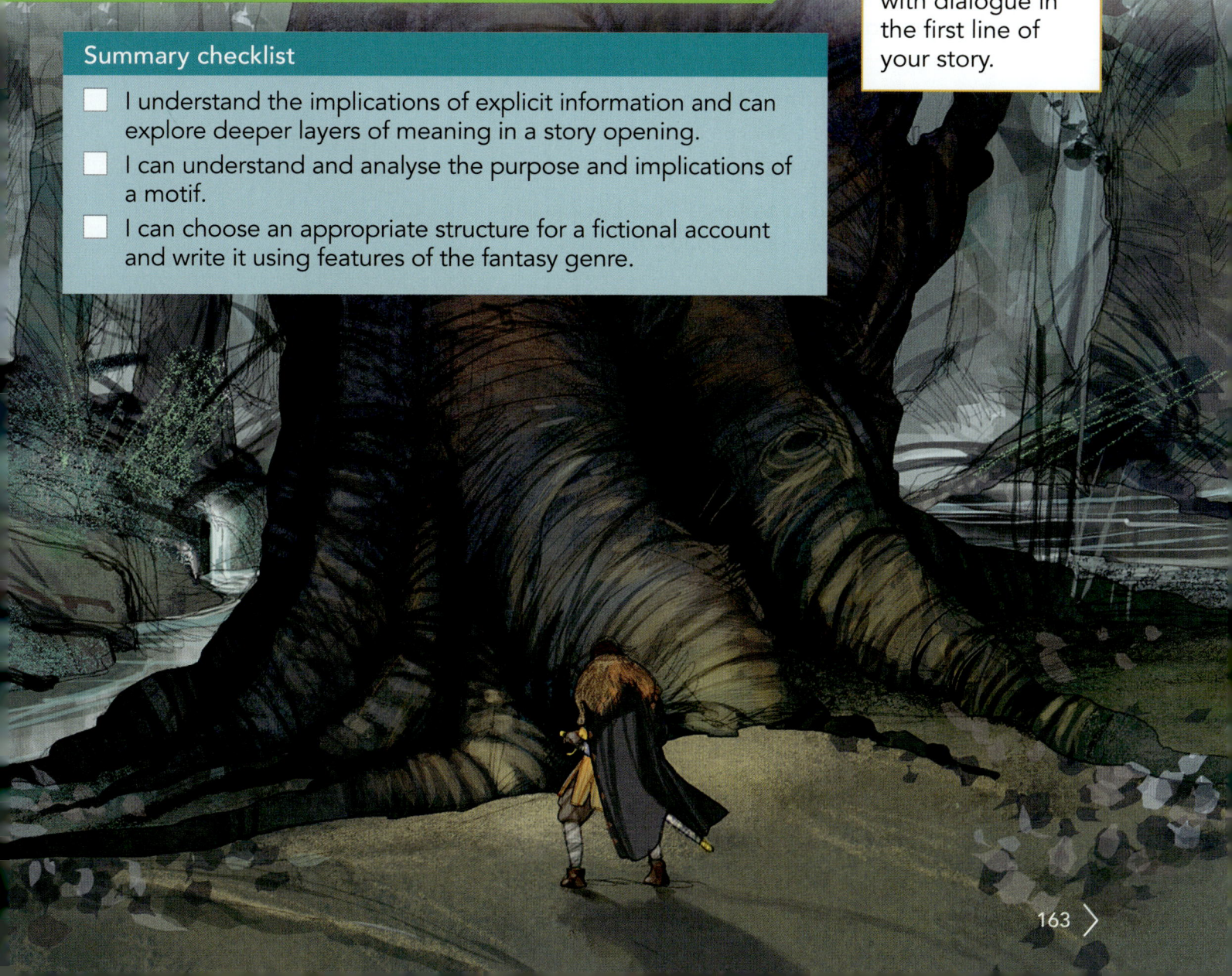

> 7.2 The farmers

In this session, you will:

- use your voice to convey character when reading an unseen text aloud
- consider the effect of formality in dialogue
- discuss themes and patterns in a fantasy story.

Getting started

In pairs, discuss all the different ways you can think of to use your voice to create different effects. To get you started, try saying this sentence in a variety of ways: *I am very much afraid that I cannot allow you to proceed, sir.*

The second part of 'The Journey Within' includes a serious conversation between Aveleen and Celegorn, and a confrontation between two farmers.

1   Read the extract aloud in groups of five. Each group member should take one of the following parts:

- narrator
- Celegorn
- Aveleen
- male farmer
- female farmer.

Read confidently, using your voice to show the relationships between the speakers and to convey the details of the events. Remember to read ahead a little to ensure you speak with accuracy.

Speaking tip

When performing dialogue, remember that you are trying to convey a relationship between the speakers. That means thinking carefully about the characters' feelings towards each other and using your voice imaginatively to convey those feelings.

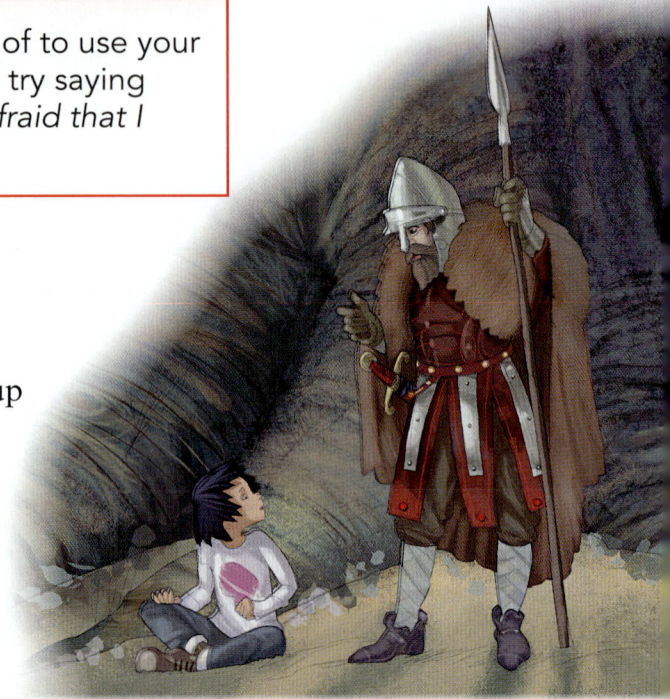

Extract 2

Celegorn had not given her many details. After spending a night beneath the Tree, he had simply announced:

'The Tree has spoken. The identity of the Chosen One is hidden in the lake at the crater of the Brown Mountain. I want you to make a journey.'

'In a lake?' Aveleen had asked. 'And why me?'

'It must be you, for I cannot trust the others not to bring back their own name.'

'Where is this lake? There is no such mountain in our land.'

'This is not a typical journey. The starting point is in the centre of the Tree. Go, get yourself ready!'

The sound of voices banished the image of Celegorn from her mind.

A few feet in front of Aveleen, the path was blocked by a pair of farmers arguing over a bundle of wheat, which was at risk of being ripped to shreds before the matter was settled.

Where could these two have come from? Were they even real? The young girl brushed these questions aside and welcomed the chance to ask about her route. They did not seem in the least surprised at seeing the traveller.

'This is the last bundle,' he said, ignoring Aveleen's query entirely. 'I need it to bake bread. There's nothing sweeter than the sound of a loaf crisping up in the oven—'

'No, we need it to make *cake*, you stupid toad,' the woman protested. 'Then we can sell 'em, and for a good price!'

Aveleen looked at the couple for a moment. Standing side by side with their hands on their hips, tight-lipped and frowning heavily, they looked almost identical, like a mirror image of each other. They reminded her of someone, but she could not think who.

'Why don't you sow your grains of wheat?' Aveleen suggested after a moment's thought. 'With a bit of patience, you'll be able to make bread *and* cake!'

The man and the woman looked the girl up and down, as if seeing her in a fresh light.

'That's not a bad idea, you know. Wise words, young lady—'

> crater: a large hollow in the ground

'You should've thought of that!' the woman yelled at her husband.

'Same for you!'

As a fresh **barrage** of insults thundered from the odd couple, Aveleen decided to continue on her way, having lost all hope that they might come to her aid. But after only a few steps, the farmers caught up with her.

'Wait!' they shouted in perfect harmony. 'You're on a false trail. If you want to reach the Brown Mountain, you must not set foot on it. You have to walk alongside it, otherwise you'll never leave the valley.'

> **barrage:** an overwhelming number of things

Language focus

'Formality' refers to how serious or relaxed the language and grammar in a text are – including word choices, use of standard English, and features such as **contractions**, punctuation and missing verbs. In non-fiction texts, a writer will usually stick to the same level of formality throughout a text, but in fiction a writer may vary the level of formality to create specific effects. This is particularly true of dialogue, where different levels of formality can convey the status, situation and feelings of different characters. As in real life, a character's dialogue can vary in formality depending on their situation.

Look at these two examples of dialogue:

- 'I am very much afraid that I cannot allow you to proceed, sir.'

- 'You're not gettin' past me!'

The first example is very formal, with words such as *proceed* and the use of *sir* as a polite term of address. There are no contractions and the line uses standard English. The overall effect is that the speaker appears respectful, controlled and maybe even a little menacing.

The second example is much less formal. A contraction (*you're*) is used, the dropped *g* from 'getting' and the exclamation all create an impression of heightened emotion and a lack of control, or perhaps aggression.

Key word

contraction: two or three words that are combined to make one shorter word with letters left out; the missing letters are indicated by an apostrophe

2   Write a 150-word analysis of the levels of formality used in the dialogue in Extract 2 of 'The Journey Within'. In your analysis, consider:

- what the dialogue between Celegorn and Aveleen suggests about their relationship

- the effect created by the dialogue between Aveleen and the two farmers.

Use examples from the text, and comment on the writer's language and punctuation choices.

3   One feature of genre is the use of the story patterns – that is, familiar events and story sequences. In fantasy texts, a familiar story pattern is the quest. This is a journey where the central character goes in search of something, facing many adventures and challenges along the way.

Write a paragraph exploring Aveleen's encounter with the farmers. Comment on:

- the problem faced by Aveleen and the farmers
- how the problem is solved and what personal qualities Aveleen shows.

4   In pairs, discuss the events of the two extracts of the story you have read so far. Using examples from the text, explore:

- what the extracts show about the theme of power in the story – who has it and how it is used
- your response to the fantasy elements in the story
- what you think will happen in the rest of the story.

Develop your discussion by exploring in depth areas where you agree or disagree. Think about how your comments shape and contribute to the discussion.

- How confident do you feel about your understanding of story patterns? Will they help you when making predictions?
- How much did your previous understanding of these features help you in the last activity?

Summary checklist

- ☐ I can read an unseen text aloud, using my voice to convey character.
- ☐ I can analyse the use and effect of formality in dialogue.
- ☐ I can contribute effectively to a discussion on themes and patterns in a fantasy story.

> 7.3 The bronze door

In this session, you will:

- explore the way time is used to structure a narrative
- consider how a theme is presented and how it relates to other texts
- explore the effect of setting on character
- describe an imaginative fantasy setting.

Getting started

Think of a place you have been that had a memorable impact on you. Then, in pairs, describe those places to each other. Try to help your partner really imagine the scene, so they understand why the place had such an impact.

Read the next part of 'The Journey Within'. Here, Aveleen finds herself in another fantastical setting.

Extract 3

Aveleen managed to abandon the path she had been stuck on for two days. But it was not too long before she became thoroughly frustrated. The slope was slippery, and the summit was still so far off . . . Would she be able to make it the whole way? She was not even sure how many days the journey was meant to last. 'It will take as much time as is necessary,' Celegorn had assured her. How could he say such a thing when the smallest delay might prevent her from **bidding him farewell**?

Aveleen hitched herself onto a small ledge as one of the suns was setting. Carved into the cliff face was a bronze door, so high that it would have loomed over the heads of the Giants from her own land.

Aveleen ran her hands over the bronze before recoiling sharply. The door was opening in the middle.

'Welcome.'

bidding him farewell: saying goodbye to him

A slender woman with big, shimmering eyes beckoned her inside. Aveleen let her bag slide to the ground and started forward, unable to offer any resistance.

Her first few paces left her stunned. She marvelled at the space, the light, the sky – how could all this exist inside a mountain? There was so much to admire that she found it hard to breathe. Trees, flowers, animals, buildings and people . . . wherever she laid her eyes, she was struck by the **exquisite** perfection around her. The feeling overwhelmed her, as though her five senses had finally realised their true purpose.

The woman gave her **garments** whose colours did not exist in her land. She then presented her with all manner of unfamiliar dishes, like desserts that were somehow both piping-hot and icy-cold, or biscuits whose texture and flavour shifted with every bite, one second as dense as a storm cloud, the next as light as sea foam.

Aveleen felt she could spend an entire lifetime exploring the wonders of this place and still not skim the surface. Time seemed to stand still. She stayed there for several days, maybe months, until the woman with the **crystalline** eyes returned to her side.

'Tomorrow, you are to become one of us. If you live with us for ever more, you will not know pain or suffering, you . . . '

Aveleen let herself be cradled by the woman's words. Her face was so reassuring, the tone of her voice so enchanting. Again there was a certain familiarity. Her face **evoked** a vague memory of Celegorn, which stirred Aveleen. How could she have forgotten her mission? They were relying on her.

She decided to leave the City.

> **exquisite:** delicate and beautiful
>
> **garments:** clothes
>
> **crystalline:** clear, like a crystal
>
> **evoked:** brought to mind

1   One of the structural features of 'The Journey Within' is the way time is used in the narrative. In the present time frame of the story, Aveleen is on her journey, but past time is also referred to in flashbacks to her conversations with Celegorn.

In pairs, discuss:

- what the brief flashback to Celegorn's words (and Aveleen's reaction to them) adds to the story

- the contrast between Aveleen's experience inside the mountain and her memory of Celegorn (consider Aveleen's decision at the end of the extract).

2   As well as being used as a narrative device, time is also a major theme in the story. In Unit 4, you explored ideas about the theme of time in some other texts, including the following:

- there are significant moments in time when a person's life changes

- humans are aware of the importance of time and how quickly time passes

- we often reflect on the past and think a lot about the future.

How are these ideas and attitudes presented in 'The Journey Within'? Write an analysis of what the story so far shows about time. Use references from the text to support your points.

3   The way the writer describes Aveleen's experiences inside the mountain helps the reader understand her amazement.

In pairs, identify and discuss:

- words and phrases that reveal Aveleen's emotions

- the use of visual, aural and tactile images

- the use of figurative language

- why she is tempted to stay, what makes her change her mind and what this reveals about her personal qualities.

4   Write your own description of a fantastical setting that creates similar emotions to those Aveleen experiences. Either write in the first-person voice or use Aveleen as the character in your description.

Your new setting could be somewhere underground, above the clouds or an idea of your own.

Use word choices, language techniques and images to bring the setting to life for your reader – someone of your own age who enjoys fantasy stories. Write about 250 words, using any strategies you know to spell complex words accurately.

Writing tip

When writing descriptively, think carefully about the emotions and feelings you are trying to create. From there, consider what sights and sounds would inspire those feelings. Do not underestimate the impact of tactile imagery – often it is less commonly used, but it can really help the reader imagine the scene.

Peer assessment

Swap descriptions with a partner. Read their draft and feed back on:

- the effectiveness of language choices (do they help you to picture the scene?)

- the accuracy of spelling (use a dictionary if you need to).

Summary checklist

- [ ] I can analyse the way time is used as a structural device in a narrative text.
- [ ] I can explain how a theme is presented and explore it in relation to other texts.
- [ ] I can comment on how setting can impact character.
- [ ] I can write a description of a fantasy setting to create specific effects.

> 7.4 The crow

In this session, you will:

- consider the significance of plot and character development
- compare the use of symbols in two texts
- explore the content of fantasy stories and readers' reactions to them
- write a monologue in the voice of a particular character.

Getting started

In groups of three, discuss any stories or films you know that feature talking animals. What do these characters add to the narrative? How do audiences normally react to them?

Now read the next part of 'The Journey Within'.

Extract 4

Aveleen had gone for several days without any boots. The mountain had rallied in its efforts to frustrate her progress, and now her soles had given way to the rocks and deserts that she had crossed. Deserts halfway up a mountain? Aveleen had lost count of how many times she thought she might die of thirst, only to stumble on a drop of water in a plant she knew from her own land. More than once she had considered turning back to the City.

What if she found nothing at the end?

But Aveleen remained resolute. She reached the crater of the Brown Mountain one cold day at dawn. She had walked through the night, unable to focus on anything except putting one foot in front of the other.

The plain below was gleaming in the setting light of the twin suns. It seemed so very distant. How many months had passed since she had left? How many green leaves could there still be on the Tree?

Just ahead, the lake in the mountain's crater sparkled like a patch of sky that had fallen from the heavens. She felt her heart pounding as she scrambled down the last of the gentle slope, her eyes never leaving the lake. A few steps away there was a fearsome rumble, and the earth began to shake beneath her feet, causing her to sink to her knees. When she opened her eyes, she saw before her a vast chasm blocking her way to the lake. After a moment's stunned silence, a mighty wave of anger tore through the young girl. Why this final obstacle when she was just feet away from completing her quest? Aveleen flung back her head and let out a howl of rage and bewilderment.

A swoosh of wings cut short her cries. Aveleen turned to see a crow staring at her, its feathers lustrous in the evening light. Straight away the bird inspired an intense dislike in her. Something in its eyes made her deeply suspicious.

> rallied: renewed its strength
> resolute: determined

> bewilderment: the feeling of being confused
> lustrous: shining

Yet again, however, the crow reminded her of someone . . . Why was she so utterly incapable of establishing who?

'Why don't you just pick the name of the Chosen One yourself, you idiot?' the crow cawed. 'You would have spared yourself the journey. Look at you, all covered in muck. I don't know if the villagers will laugh or cry when you tell them about your miserable failure.'

1   Make notes on:

- the external and internal challenges Aveleen faces

- the things that help and encourage her on the quest

- how the appearance of the crow changes the mood of the story at this point.

2   In pairs, discuss what this part of the story reveals about Aveleen. How does it add to what you know about her character already?

3   In Session 6.3 you read 'Chasm', in which a chasm was used to symbolise the distance between two people in a family relationship.

In pairs, compare the symbol of the chasm to the crater that Aveleen encounters. What is the crater's significance?

4   Fantasy stories often present situations that may not be possible in the real world, but which echo real situations. For example, in real life people often face crucial decisions that shape the course of their life. Such events may be shown in fantasy stories, except in this form of fiction, the nature of the situation is fantastical.

In 'The Journey Within', Aveleen has so far met two farmers, a woman in a beautiful mountain world and a talking crow. She has noticed something familiar about all these characters. In pairs, discuss:

- the attitudes and actions of these strange characters

- what happens in their interactions with Aveleen

- why the writer may have included these characters and interactions.

Reading tip

Remember that objects in stories sometimes have a symbolic meaning that represents an idea or an aspect of a character's personality. However, remember too that often objects in stories are literal things – do not try to interpret everything symbolically!

5   People's preferences and opinions influence the way they react to stories. Below are two views about 'The Journey Within'.

a   In pairs, discuss the two views. Which parts, if any, do you agree with? Why?

b   Discuss your own opinions of the story so far. Which parts have you enjoyed?

c   Write a summary of the different views you have discussed.

> I don't really enjoy fantasy very much, but I do like the mysteriousness of the story – especially the fact that you're not sure whether Aveleen is really experiencing these things, or whether it's some kind of dream. I'm less impressed by the appearance of the talking crow – it seems too odd and a bit childish!

> Fantasy is my favourite genre. The best fantasy stories allow you to connect with the human qualities of the main character, and that's what happens in 'The Journey Within'. She seems normal. I also like the way the various other characters she meets all have symbolic qualities.

Speaking tip

When you give an opinion, remember to explain *why* you think what you do. Explain your own preferences and the contexts that influence your view. Use the text under discussion to support the specific points you make.

Peer assessment

Think about the way your partner gave their opinion in this discussion.

•   How effectively did they explain their own preferences – did you understand why they felt the way they did?

•   How well did they use the text to support their views – did they give helpful references from the story?

6 Imagine you are Aveleen. Write a script of a **monologue** in which you explain how you feel about your journey. It should begin at the point just before the appearance of the crow, when you are in despair.

In your monologue, comment on:

- the confusion you feel
- your thoughts about Celegorn
- your feelings about the journey so far.

Remember that a monologue is written to entertain the reader or listener, so make it dramatic and appealing through your choice of words and variety of sentence structures.

Start by thinking about the voice you will use for Aveleen and how you can show her conflicting feelings. You could include stage directions and sound effects if you wish. Write around 300 words in fluent handwriting.

Key word

monologue: a story or speech given by one character

Summary checklist

- [ ] I can comment on how plot and characters are developed in a story and what this means.
- [ ] I can identify the meaning of symbols and compare how they are used in different texts.
- [ ] I can respond to readers' reactions about the content of fantasy stories, and express my own response.
- [ ] I can write a monologue in the voice of a character to entertain the reader.

> 7.5 Nothing

In this session, you will:

- work out the meaning of unfamiliar words
- consider the structural effect of anti-climax
- explore how beliefs about life are reflected in a text
- discuss and analyse the theme of nature.

Getting started

What do you understand by the words 'fortune' and 'fate' in the phrases below? In small groups, discuss what different meanings and connotations these words have.

- My car cost a fortune.
- I had the good fortune to meet my hero.
- It was fate that we met each other.
- He suffered a horrible fate.

Read the next part of 'The Journey Within'.

1   Six words in the extract are underlined. As you read, use any appropriate strategies you know to work out the meaning of the words. Check your answers with a partner.

Extract 5

The crow still stared at Aveleen with mocking eyes.

'Unless . . . unless I go on your behalf? Here, give me your gold necklace and I'll take care of it.'

Aveleen was so <u>incredulous</u> she wanted to burst out laughing.

A large golden ladybird chose that very moment to land on Aveleen's hand. The girl watched as it took off again and settled a few inches from the <u>precipice</u>. Then something happened.

Instead of making a turn, the ladybird carried on straight ahead, before <u>zigzagging</u> across the <u>void</u>. At first, Aveleen thought her weary body was making her see things. But as clear as day, the ladybird was standing in the middle of the chasm.

Aveleen approached the gap and, still on her knees, started tapping it.

It was quite incredible . . . she could see the chasm, but in several places, she felt firm ground too.

The Tree had protected her people **since time immemorial**. It was unthinkable that she had been led to a dead end. There had to be a way to reach the lake. There had to be.

Aveleen started ripping handfuls of wild grass from the ground. It was only when she saw the two piles that had formed either side of her that she had the idea.

She stood up slowly and threw the first lot onto the precipice.

The grass marked out a path.

Aveleen shoved the rest of it into her leather pack. Her heart racing, she placed a foot on the green walkway as the crow flew off.

There it was.

The Lake sparkled like a silver fish. Aveleen caught sight of her reflection in the water. She brought a hand to her cheek. She seemed different.

As Aveleen entered the cold water, her clothes drifted around her like broken wings. She emerged from the depths hours later with a sense of emptiness. There was nothing at the bottom of the lake.

Nothing.

> Beneath the **algae**
>
> > there was nothing but
>
> > > fine sand.

On the bank, Aveleen curled up to regain some warmth. She fell into a deep sleep, <u>oblivious</u> to the rolling sky over her head that was about to <u>engulf</u> her.

> **since time immemorial:** for a very long time – beyond memory

> **algae:** a green water plant

2 Often, fantasy stories build to a **climax** towards the end – a moment of drama where the central character has to prove themselves before they enjoy success. However, in this extract of 'The Journey Within', the writer uses an **anti-climax**: Aveleen discovers that there is nothing in the lake.

Write a 100-word analysis of the effect of this structural choice.

- What effect does the event have on:
  - the reader
  - the character?
- What does it lead you to expect will happen next, in the final part of the story?

3 Fantasy stories are often set in unusual worlds and times. However, these may still have rules, beliefs and ways of life that are similar to real life. Two popular beliefs about the way real life works are:

- Fortune – the idea that luck or chance affects our lives.
- Fate – the idea that an unseen power guides our lives.

To what extent are these beliefs reflected in 'The Journey Within'? In pairs, consider all the things that have happened to Aveleen so far. Discuss the extent to which her journey:

- is a series of chance meetings and good/bad luck
- seems to be guided by an unseen power.

> **Key words**
>
> **climax:** the most exciting or important part of something
>
> **anti-climax:** a point in a story where expectations of success or a dramatic event are overturned and a character experiences disappointment instead

> **Speaking tip**
>
> When discussing how texts reflect belief systems, remember that different cultures and individuals have their own views about how life works. Always be respectful of other people's beliefs when discussing these complex topics.

- What were the challenges of identifying how beliefs are reflected in a text?
- How effective and respectful was your discussion?

4   Nature is a prominent theme in 'The Journey Within' – many natural objects and animals appear in the story. In small groups:

a   make a list of all the different aspects of nature that Aveleen encounters

b   discuss whether nature helps or hinders Aveleen on her journey

c   explore what the writer shows about the relationship between humans and the natural world; is this a positive depiction of that relationship?

Explore your ideas in detail, using appropriate language.

5   Now write an analysis of nature in the story. You should explore:

•   the significance of the Tree

•   the interactions Aveleen has with natural items and animals

•   the extent to which nature influences Aveleen's actions.

Write 250 words using formal, standard English.

Summary checklist

☐ I can choose appropriate strategies to work out the meaning of unfamiliar words.

☐ I can explain the effect of an anti-climax on a text.

☐ I can comment on how beliefs about life, including fate and fortune, are reflected in a text.

☐ I can discuss the theme of nature in a text and then write a formal analysis.

> 7.6 Chosen One

In this session, you will:

- express your reactions to the ending of the story
- discuss whether the story fits the genre of *Bildungsroman*
- listen to the views of others about the full story
- write your own fantasy story.

Getting started

On your own, note down your predictions about the ending of 'The Journey Within'. What will happen to the main characters? Will it be a happy or sad ending? Then get together in pairs and compare your ideas.

Read the final part of 'The Journey Within'.

Extract 6

Aveleen woke with a jolt and immediately made herself remember. The Lake. She must have missed a clue, some stone, or a piece of wood that had gone unnoticed with the name engraved on it.

She opened her eyes abruptly, but the scream she wanted to **unleash** stayed in her throat.

What was she doing in her house?

Celegorn was facing her, hunched over more than ever. Old age had suddenly caught up with him; his body seemed completely **dilapidated**. Aveleen felt tears in her eyes. She was not sure if it was sorrow at seeing her father in that state, joy at being reunited with him or fury that she had come home without a name.

'Tell me what you saw up there', Celegorn said.

unleash: to let out
dilapidated: run down, looking very old or neglected

Aveleen disappeared into the depths of her memory. The crow, the chasm, the bottom of the lake, the cold, the weeds.

'So you did not see a single face?' Celegorn asked.

Aveleen shook her head vigorously. Apart from her reflection in the surface, there had been nothing.

Her father was now giving her an unusual look.

Aveleen felt as if the blood was draining from her body. Yes, she had seen a face in the lake.

Her own.

She was numb. Could she be the Chosen One?

'I have always believed in you,' Celegorn continued. 'But when it became clear that you would not offer yourself to the Tree, I knew I had to help you realise who you are, who you have been since you were young. I watched you throughout your journey. You showed wisdom, loyalty and great courage. You were able to make difficult decisions. Do you remember?'

'So this quest was your idea? The Tree never said that the name was at the summit? But if that's the case, how can you be sure that I am the Chosen One?'

'There is not much time,' Celegorn said in his quiet voice. 'You have been gone seven days, and only a few leaves remain on the Tree. If you feel it within you, then come.'

Aveleen passed through the whispering crowd. No woman had ever put herself forward.

But when the Tree, their protector, embraced the girl in its branches, illuminating her with a silver halo, no one could question the identity of their new guide.

Aveleen looked up at them and smiled.

Now she knew that it was her.

And she was ready.

> **vigorously:** with energy
>
> **illuminating:** lighting up
>
> **halo:** a circle of light above the head

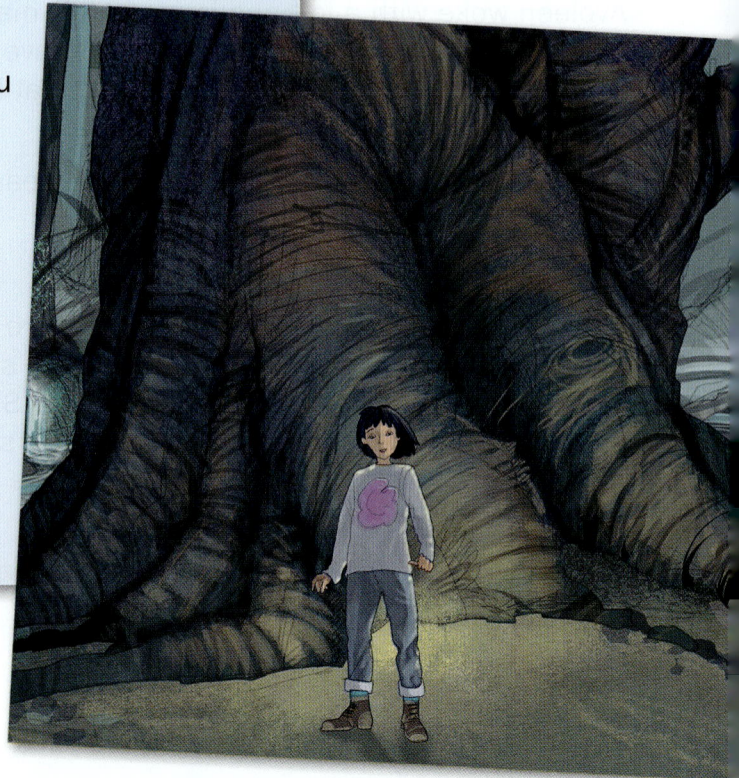

1   In pairs, discuss your reactions to the ending of the story. Consider:

- whether the ending was what you expected, and if you found it satisfying

- what the ending suggests about the power of the Tree

- whether this is a sad or happy ending.

2   'The Journey Within' could be seen as an example of a *Bildungsroman* – a text that shows how a young person matures into an adult. *Bildungsroman* texts typically focus on a character facing challenges that help them mature and accept their role as an adult.

In pairs, discuss:

- whether this description accurately describes Aveleen's experiences, and why

- the significance of the story's title.

> **Key word**
>
> *Bildungsroman:* a type of story that focuses on the moral development of a young person as they grow to adulthood

3   You are going to hear four learners give their interpretation of what 'The Journey Within' means. As you listen, make specific notes on:

a   Jack's views about the minor characters in the story

b   Omar's views about gender and power issues

c   Mana's views about nature and humans

d   Laura's views about Celegorn.

> **Listening tip**
>
> When people are talking about complex ideas like this, listen very carefully to the explanation given and be very specific about what you write down. Try to isolate the key point a speaker is making, rather than trying to note down every detail.

4   In groups of three or four, discuss your reactions to the views you have just heard. Which ones did you feel best reflected your own views about the story?

Remember to organise your discussion carefully, taking turns to respond and using the expertise within your group in the most productive way possible.

5 You are now going to write your own short fantasy story. It should feature a young character on a journey, showing how they learn and develop along the way.

Choose your own fantasy setting and other imaginative characters. Use the skills and knowledge about the genre that you have developed in this unit, making effective language, structure and content choices that will appeal to a teenage reader.

Write about 500 words.

Writing tip

When planning a full story, think carefully about how it will end. Often, it can be effective to decide how the story will conclude, then work backwards from that point.

Peer assessment

Swap drafts with a partner and check the effectiveness of the following.

- **Characterisation**: is the central character interesting enough to appeal to the audience?
- Plot: are the story events engaging?
- Language and structure: what advice can you give about improving these aspects?

Edit and redraft your work before submitting it to your teacher. Make sure your phrasing and spelling are accurate.

Key word

characterisation: how a writer conveys a character's nature and personality

---

Summary checklist

- [ ] I can comment in detail on the ending of a story.
- [ ] I can identify the genre features of *Bildungsroman* in a story.
- [ ] I can understand and respond to the views expressed by others about a text.
- [ ] I can write my own fantasy story using appropriate literary, language and structural techniques.

Check your progress

Answer the following questions.

1   Explain, using examples, what a motif is. How does it differ from a symbol?

2   Give a detailed account of the differences between formal and informal English.

3   Using examples, explain the significance of time as a structural device.

4   'Fantasy stories often present situations that may not be possible in the real world, but which echo real situations.' Explain what this means in your own words, using an example.

5   What are climaxes and anti-climaxes and what effect do they have on the reader's experience of a story?

6   What is the general pattern of a *Bildungsroman* text?

Project

In groups, you are going to come up with some ideas for a new television series – a fantasy story that runs for ten episodes.

Long-running fantasy television shows contain many of the features you have studied in this unit, such as quests and magical creatures. As well as several different settings, they also feature family groups or tribes, who may be in conflict with each other. The plots are often about power and control, and they contain many different types of people with different statuses and titles.

Start by discussing and making notes about the world in which you will set your story. Decide on:

* the name of the world and its typical landscapes, settings and climate
* the central characters – you will need to make them distinctive and think carefully about the role they perform, such as hero or villain
* the families, tribes, creatures and minor characters that appear
* the main sources of conflict or problems, and the purpose of any quests.

Continued

Once you have these general ideas, start to think about the plot, including any dramatic moments or romantic elements you could include. You could discuss:

- the overall plot across the ten episodes – what is the main point of conflict and how does it end?

- ideas for one or two individual episodes

- the **backstory** of the main characters – a brief **biography**

- ideas for costumes and music.

Present your ideas to the class as imaginatively as possible using talk, drawings or even drama to show them your ideas. Undertake group roles as you see fit and present your ideas confidently.

Key words

backstory: the fictional history or background created for a character in a story or film

biography: an account of someone's life

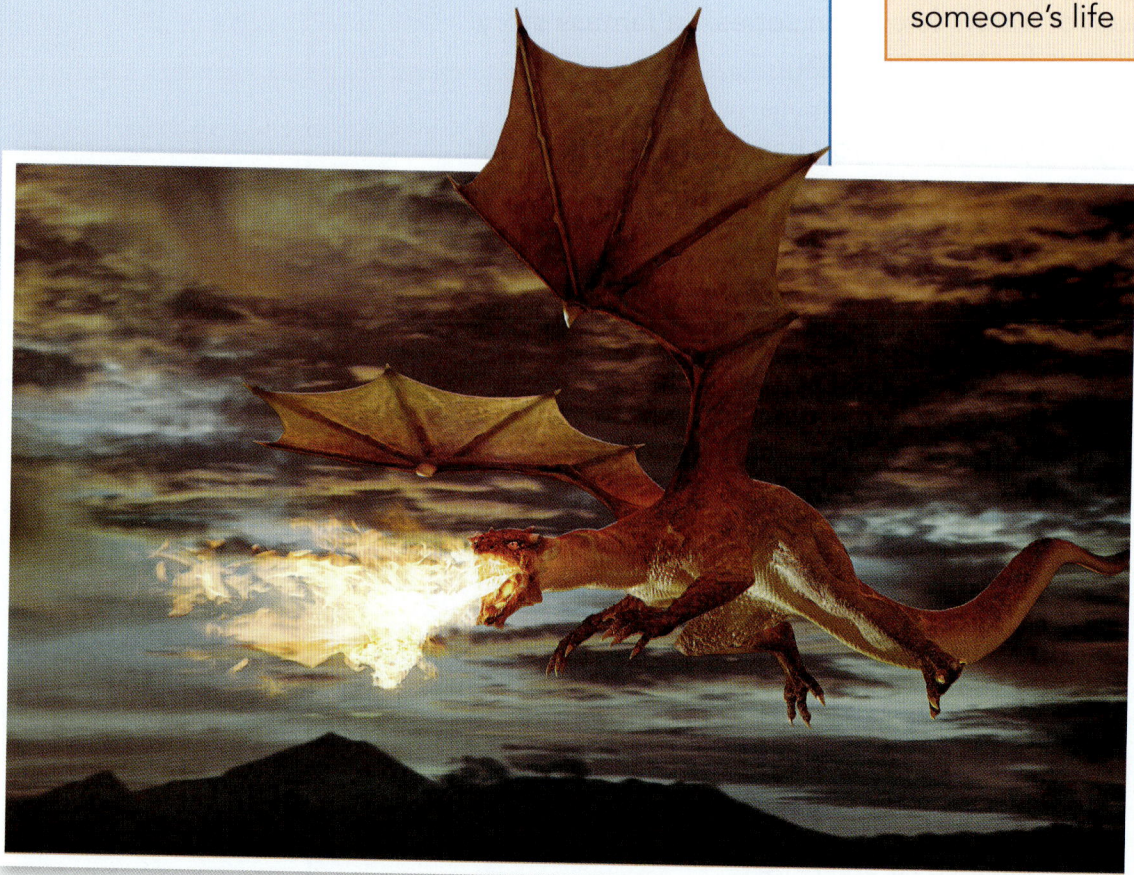

8 > Different lives

In this unit, you will study texts about different lives and experiences. You will explore a play set in Zimbabwe, read a speech by a famous actor and consider issues about disability. You will also read and write part of a science-fiction story.

> 8.1 The aeroplane

In this session, you will:

- use voice and movement to convey dramatic ideas
- explore how physical action, set design and symbol show character and theme
- consider the way conflict is shown through language choices.

Getting started

In pairs, discuss interesting sets you have seen used in films. What made them interesting and did they have any connection with the themes of the film?

I Want to Fly

I Want to Fly by Thembelihle Moyo is a play set in Zimbabwe. One of its main themes is social inequality, which is explored through the representation of two different lifestyles – the poor rural lives of 18-year-old Yinka and her mother, Mankwiji, and the more privileged people of Zimbabwe. In spite of her background, Yinka wants a different life – she wants to be a pilot.

1   Work in pairs.

    a   Read the following extract aloud, focusing on reading accurately and confidently.

    b   Discuss how the set design reflects the main theme of the play.

Extract 1

The story has two settings in juxtaposition, one represents the rich and the other the poor.

The poor area is depicted by a reed mat and a rolled up torn blanket. Traditional African huts are painted on canvas cloth, emphasizing the period where poor rural folks were still building their homes using mud.

The second area depicts a wealthier lifestyle – the painting on the canvas shows two quality chairs and a round table. Modern houses also add a touch of the rich lifestyle of these people in the canvas painting.

The curtains open and YINKA *is on the stage, miming flying like a bird, using her arms.*

YINKA   (*recites the poem in a rich strong voice*)
         I want to fly like an eagle, fly high and far
         Using my **flamboyant** wings and I will let
         The winds blow me away. As far away from
         Home as possible. I want to fly and visit those
         Places I always dream of, I want to fly.

YINKA *looks in the direction of the wealthy setting as she picks up a handmade aeroplane from the ground where a magazine about aeroplanes is lying. She picks the magazine up, looks at it, and she pauses.*

> **flamboyant:** confident and stylish

MANKWINJI, YINKA'S *mother, appears from the right wing limping slowly towards her daughter.*

MANKWINJI   My daughter how far can you go?

              The hunters have already laid a trap for you

              You won't be able to fly high; your wings will
              be broken,

              You are already destined to remain in this
              village and you shall plough

              Back your fruits to this village not to any other.

She pauses and looks in her daughter's direction as YINKA *playfully flies her plane and* MANKWINJI *swings into action. Shaking her head and moving towards her daughter.*

MANKWINJI   How many times must I to tell you to stop
              dreaming, haa? You always want to irritate your
              father Nqwayi with small issues, throw away
              that **gadget**, will you?

YINKA *picks up her magazine and holds it tight in her arms, with her aeroplane.*

YINKA   No Mama I won't, this is my dream and it means
              so much to me.

MANKWINJI *moves closer to her slowly but intentionally, eyeing* YINKA'S *magazine.*

MANKWINJI   Have you started preparing the evening meal,
              Yinka?

YINKA *frowns and shakes her head.* MANKWINJI *grabs the miniature aeroplane and throws it to the far end of the stage.* YINKA *rushes to pick it up on the verge of screaming.*

YINKA   I made it Mama, it's my passion.

MANKWINJI *breathes out loudly and paces up and down the room in confusion.*

> **gadget:** a small device or tool, often electronic

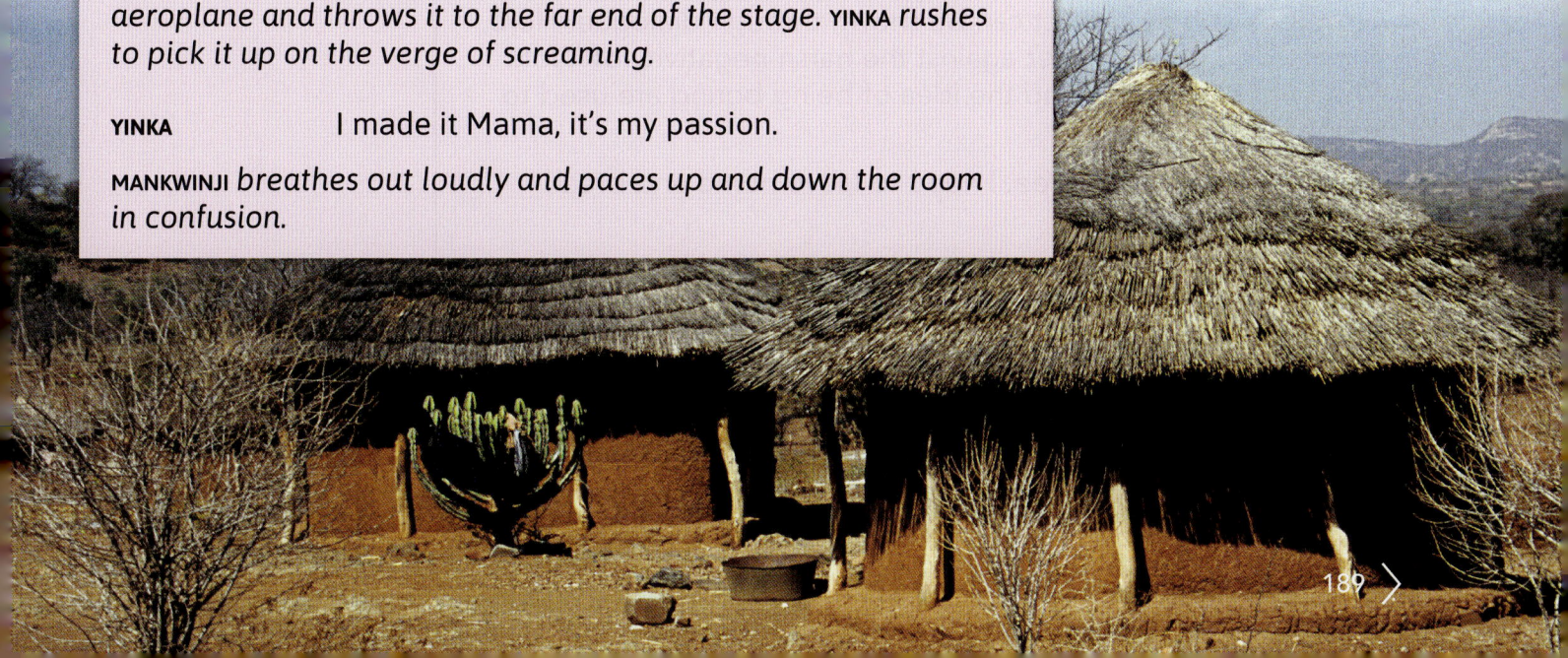

2   Now act out the scene in pairs, using your voice and movement to show the characters and ideas being explored in the play. Try to show how Yinka and her mother each feel, and the relationship between then.

3   Physical actions and symbols are both effective ways to reveal aspects of character and theme in drama. On your own, make notes on the following questions.

   a   What do Yinka and Mankwinji's physical actions suggest about their personalities and experiences?

   b   How does the set design establish the main theme of social inequality? What does the playwright suggest about life in Zimbabwe?

   c   How do the title of the play and the symbol of flight reflect Yinka's ambitions?

Speaking tip

When acting out a scene, remember to use movement and gesture to convey character. The stage directions will give you some information, but you will also need to decide other issues, such as how you stand and how you interact with other actors.

Language focus

Conflict is the driving force in stories – every narrative needs a problem or situation for the main character to overcome. Conflicts are expressed in the overall plot, but they can also be conveyed in language choices.

Consider the words and images in these stage directions from a play about mining. Notice how the image of the cramped mine, shown in words such as 'dark' and 'enclosed', is contrasted with a sense of freedom reflected in words such as 'wide, green lawn'.

*   The set allows the audience to see the dark, enclosed underground world of the miners and also the large house of the mine owner, with its wide, green lawn and apple trees.

Now look at how conflict can be shown through dialogue. Here, the words 'I need' are set against the harsh negativity of 'No!'. The symbol of chains and the idea of being bound are used to emphasis the conflict.

ARJAN   I need to be free. I need to leave home and break these chains.

DANIELA   No! Your place is here. You are bound to this family for life.

4   Write an analysis of how language is used to present different types of conflict in the extract from *I Want to Fly*. Explore the conflict between:

- the two lifestyles implied in the set design

- Yinka's ambitions and the world she lives in

- Yinka and Mankwinji.

Summary checklist

☐ I can read and perform a play extract, using voice and movement to convey dramatic ideas.

☐ I understand how physical action, set design and symbol convey theme.

☐ I can analyse the way conflict is shown in language choices.

› 8.2 Mrs Manzi

In this session, you will:

- read a scene from a play aloud in pairs

- explore the way relationships between characters are presented

- compare how contrasting characters are presented

- write a drama scene featuring contrasting characters.

Getting started

In pairs, discuss the positive ways that adults help and inspire young people. Use these pictures to start your discussion. Which adults have helped you during your life?

In the next extract from *I Want to Fly*, Yinka meets Mrs Manzi, her chemistry teacher. Mrs Manzi encourages Yinka to think about her future.

1 Read the scene aloud in pairs. Try to read confidently and with expression. Read ahead where necessary.

58

Extract 2

Store room set up with desk and two chairs.

MRS MANZI, YINKA's chemistry teacher, in her early thirties, is seated in her store room, marking, when YINKA knocks on the door. She looks up and smiles at her.

MRS MANZI	Oh Yinka, you can come through, how was the maths paper my dear?
YINKA	It was fine **Ma'am**; rumour has it that you are going away, in fact transferring to town.
MRS MANZI	You are writing your finals and I hope you will pass, you are one of my top students and it was great to have you in my class.

YINKA shyly smiles at her teacher.

MRS MANZI	If you do well in your maths and science subjects you might stand a chance to get a STEM **bursary**.
YINKA	What is STEM Ma'am?

YINKA is a little bit confused.

MRS MANZI	Science, Technology, Engineering and Mathematics. It is a new bursary which the government has introduced. You might stand a chance, considering your background and intelligence.

MRS MANZI says this with a smile on her face.

YINKA	Who is going to help me with the application?

MRS MANZI scribbles something on the paper and hands it to YINKA.

> **Ma'am:** a polite term of address to an older female
>
> **bursary:** a grant given to a student

YINKA	What is this supposed to mean Ma'am?
MRS MANZI	This is my home contact address; you could pay me a visit when you have collected your results. I have a feeling that you will be going to the air force college. I am sure you like flying, isn't it?
YINKA	Yes Ma'am, you guessed right. I have to go now, I am writing my chemistry paper this afternoon.
MRS MANZI	You have my support all the way. Excuse me, I too have to go, I am **invigilating** the first formers.

She remarks as she follows YINKA *off stage.*

> **invigilating:** supervising learners during an exam

- How well has your ability to read unseen texts aloud developed during this year?
- How confident do you feel with this skill?

2 In this scene, Yinka talks with another older woman. But she clearly has a different type of relationship with Mrs Manzi than she does with her mother.

Answer the following questions.

    a Make notes on the level of formality shown in the dialogue. What does this reveal about the characters' relationship?

    b Using examples from the scene, explain how the writer shows that Mrs Manzi can be seen as a role model for Yinka.

3 In *I Want to Fly*, Mrs Manzi and Mankwinji (Yinka's mother) are shown as contrasting characters.

In groups of three or four, discuss the following questions.

    a What similarities and differences are there between these two characters?

    b Why might the writer have included these characters – what themes emerge from their contrasting lives and experiences?

    c To what extent do you think the writer is criticising Yinka's mother and her attitudes?

Explore these issues fully, especially points of agreement and disagreement.

The extracts from *I Want to Fly* show two different experiences: Yinka's home life and her school life. The set design you read about in Extract 1 also gives a glimpse of the more privileged lifestyle that some people enjoy. Shumba and his wife Sihle (Yinka's aunt) are two of the wealthy characters in the play. Read the descriptions of them below.

> **SHUMBA**, a wealthy, big man who loves fashion and riches. He is a hypocrite.
>
> **AUNT SIHLE**, a kind-hearted character who has many secrets. She loves to help her brother, Yinka's father.

4 In pairs, discuss these character descriptions. Consider:

    • what the description of Shumba implies about rich people

    • the suggested contrast between Shumba's values and those of Aunt Sihle

- what storylines might emerge from the details given about these two characters.

5 You are now going to write a scene featuring Shumba and Aunt Sihle, set in their expensive home. Use dialogue and stage directions to highlight their contrasting characters. Remember that drama is based on conflict, so start by thinking what might happen in the scene to show the different attitudes of the characters. Perhaps they have different views about Yinka's education, or perhaps Sihle wants to help her family, but Shumba refuses.

Use the layout conventions of play scripts, including stage directions. Experiment with different ways of structuring the scene, and use language appropriate to the characters. Write around 350 words.

You could use these opening stage directions:

SHUMBA, *dressed in a beautiful blue suit and highly polished shoes, enters. He walks slowly and proudly – he seems very pleased with himself. He sits down in an expensive chair.* **SIHLE** *enters from the other side of the stage. She is dressed more casually.* **SIHLE** *sits down opposite her husband and he looks up.*

> **Writing tip**
>
> Although dialogue and movement are essential parts of drama, do not forget that plot is also important! In any scene, something must develop or change, so bear this in mind as you plan your scene.

Peer assessment

In pairs, read each other's scripts aloud. Offer feedback the following.

- The way the characters' personalities are conveyed – are they different and interesting enough?
- The plot – is there a convincing conflict shown?

Summary checklist

☐ I can read an unseen script aloud with confidence and expression.
☐ I can analyse the way that relationships between characters are presented in drama.
☐ I can comment on the representation of two contrasting characters.
☐ I can write a drama scene featuring contrasting characters.

> 8.3 A different voice

In this session, you will:

- listen to and answer questions about people's experiences of being disabled
- explore the content, structure, viewpoint and effects of an informative article
- consider how narrative viewpoint affects a text
- write a feature article on the subject of disabled people.

Getting started

In groups, discuss the ways in which disabled people are represented in the media and in fictional texts. What range of qualities and skills are they shown to have?

1   Listen to the audio recording of three people talking about their experiences of being disabled people. Make notes as you listen, then write full answers to these questions.

   a   What does Alisha say her main challenges are?

   b   How does Larry feel about representations of disabled people in the media?

   c   How do you react to Hamid's account of his life?

Listening tip

Remember that listening skills are not only about identifying facts; they also include thinking about how you respond to information. When considering your response to a spoken text, try to identify what words or detail made you react in the way that you did.

A perfect life

Read the following extract from an article by Rosaleen Moriarty-Simmonds, who was born with damage to her limbs.

Just Crash Through It . . .

At 45, I am a happy wife, an adoring mum, a successful business-woman, an artist – constantly busy and totally content.

I also have little legs which end above the knee but with feet, and from each shoulder I have two fingers.

When I was born I was taken away abruptly from my mother, who was only 18, but when they eventually handed me to her an unbreakable bond was formed.

Whatever barriers we came across it was as a family. Wherever the family went, I went.

Between the ages of four and 14, I went to a school for disabled children. From there I went on to college and gained a business qualification.

I had first laid eyes on the man who would become my husband when we were three years old. We continued to bump into each other and kept in touch as friends.

By our mid-twenties we had both graduated and settled into jobs. Stephen (who is also **Thalidomide** impaired) phoned me to invite me to a restaurant. We got engaged in 1987 and married a year later.

I had wanted to grow up, get married, have a family and live happily ever after. Some members of the medical profession and even family members expressed the view that I probably wouldn't be able to have children, and some even said I shouldn't.

While trying to come to terms with the prospect of being childless, the miracle happened. Just before Christmas we discovered I was pregnant. We were both **ecstatic** and **petrified**.

He arrived on 10 August. I was pretty much out of it when they first put him by me, but I recall this beautiful little face with big blue eyes looking at me and I said 'Hello James, my beautiful little boy', and then I blanked out.

From about 15-months-old he went to nursery, so his little friends got used to me very quickly. By the time he started school he was very confident and made lots of friends.

Inevitably some kids would stare and ask James questions but I had made an arrangement that if the school felt these questions were getting too complicated for him to answer, they would allow me in to talk to the children. I did this and had a wonderful afternoon with 66 five-year-olds.

Thalidomide: a sleeping tablet given to pregnant women during the 1950s-60s that caused babies to be born disabled

ecstatic: extremely happy
petrified: extremely scared

2   Make notes on:

  • the challenges Rosaleen Moriarty-Simmonds faced and how she overcame them

  • the different emotions she describes during the article

  • your impression of Rosaleen.

3   In pairs, discuss your reactions to the way the article is written.

  a   How would you describe the voice of the writer?

  b   What is the effect of the first-person perspective? How does it help the reader understand issues about disability and disabled people?

  c   What is the impact of the opening sentence and the chronological account of Rosaleen's life?

  d   What is the overall effect of the article?

  • Do you think your group explored the topic sensitively?
  • What factors influenced the quality of your discussion?

> **Speaking tip**
>
> When discussing potentially sensitive topics such as disability, remember that other learners may have friends and family members who have personal experience of such issues. Always be kind and respectful.

4   In any writing, the choice of perspective can create different details and effects. For example, an autobiographical text can include the full sweep of the writer's life, whereas biographical accounts offer an observer's perspective.

  In pairs, discuss how the account of Rosaleen's experiences might differ if it was written from the point of view of her son or her husband. Which parts of her life might they focus on? How do you think they would describe her?

5   Imagine that an online magazine has asked you to write a **feature article** that presents a positive account of disability. The magazine is aimed at teenagers and young adults. In the article, you want to show that disabled people enjoy fulfilling lives.

  Use details from the extract, information from the audio in Activity 1 and any other sources you can find. Your article should include:

  • interesting details about the positive experiences of disabled people

> **Key words**
>
> feature article: an article that discusses a particular topic in depth

- an opening paragraph that immediately captures readers' attention

- organisational features such as subheadings and a headline that sums up the main idea of the article

- quotations from Rosaleen's article

- a closing paragraph that summarises the main point of the article.

Write 400 words in standard English. Think carefully about level of formality you will use – make language and sentence structures suitable for your purpose and audience. Present your article in a way that will engage your readers.

Writing tip

Feature articles are different from news articles. They are informative, but their purpose is also to entertain. So, think carefully about how to maintain your readers' interest – how will you ensure that they want to keep reading?

Summary checklist

☐ I can listen to, make notes on and explain people's experiences of disability from an audio.

☐ I can explain the effects of content, structure and viewpoint in an informative article.

☐ I understand how different narrative viewpoints affect a text.

☐ I can write an engaging feature article, making appropriate structure and language choices.

› 8.4 He for she

Getting started

In pairs, discuss the challenges experienced by young people as they grow up. Do boys and girls experience similar or different pressures? Why do you think that is?

Gender equality

The following speech was given by Emma Watson, an actor best known for her role in the *Harry Potter* films. In the speech, she discusses issues of gender equality. Watson gave this speech in 2014 at the headquarters of the United Nations (UN). It was seen in many countries around the world.

Gender equality is your issue too

Today we are launching a campaign called 'HeForShe'.

I am reaching out to you because I need your help. We want to end **gender inequality** – and to do that we need everyone to be involved: we want to try and **galvanise** as many men and boys as possible to be **advocates** for gender equality.

I think it is right that as a woman I am paid the same as my male **counterparts**. I think it is right that I am afforded the same respect as men. But sadly I can say that there is no one country in the world where all women can expect to receive these rights.

Men – I would like to take this opportunity to extend your formal invitation. Gender equality is your issue too.

Because to date, I've seen my father's role as a parent being valued less by society.

I've seen young men suffering from mental illness unable to ask for help for fear it would make them look less 'macho'. Men don't have the benefits of equality either.

We don't often talk about men being imprisoned by gender stereotypes but I can see that they are and that when they are free, things will change for women as a natural consequence.

Both men and women should feel free to be sensitive. Both men and women should feel free to be strong.

If we stop defining each other by what we are not and start defining ourselves by what we are – we can all be freer and this is what HeForShe is about. It's about freedom.

I want men to take up this **mantle**. So their daughters, sisters and mothers can be free from prejudice but also so that their sons have permission to be vulnerable and human too.

Because the reality is that if we do nothing it will take 75 years, or for me to be nearly a hundred before women can expect to be paid the same as men for the same work. And at current rates it won't be until 2086 before all rural African girls will be able to receive a secondary education.

If you believe in equality, I applaud you.

I am inviting you to step forward, to be seen to speak up, to be the 'he' for 'she'. And to ask yourself if not me, who? If not now, when?

Thank you.

---

gender inequality: a lack of fairness or balance between men and women

galvanise: to provoke into action

advocates: supporters

counterparts: equals

---

mantle: important role

1 Work in pairs.

a Make a list of the main points Watson makes – what are the strands of her argument?

b Discuss your reactions to these points – do you agree with them?

c Discuss how people might react to this speech. For example, do you think that different genders or older people would react in different ways or not?

2 This speech was given to launch a campaign, but it was also intended to persuade people to support gender equality.

You have explored the features of persuasive texts before. Here, the persuasive techniques are quite subtle. In pairs, identify the following features and discuss how effective they are in persuading the audience to agree with the writer's ideas:

- using someone famous as the spokesperson for a topic
- implying the audience's power and the speaker's lack of it
- addressing the audience politely
- giving examples of existing inequality/unfairness
- outlining the benefits of change
- using metaphorical images
- using powerful, emotive words and concepts
- posing questions and challenges to the audience.

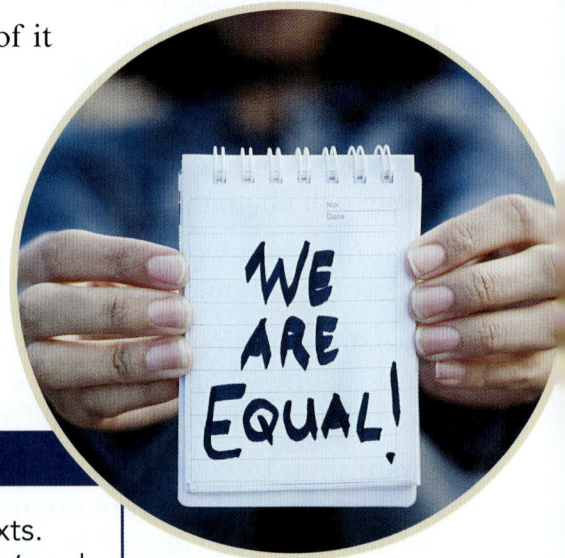

Language focus

Choices of pronouns can be very effective in persuasive texts. For example, first-person singular pronouns, such as 'I', 'me' and 'my', make the speaker or writer sound direct and sincere:

- I am really saddened by what I have seen.

In this line, the speaker makes it clear that they have been personally affected, which is effective in convincing the audience that the speaker genuinely cares about the issue.

First-person plural pronouns, such as 'we', and second person pronouns, such as 'you', can have different effects:

> ## Continued
>
> - We need to work together to change things.
>
> - We want you to help.
>
> In the first example, 'we' includes the audience, making it seem as if the speaker and audience are on the same side. In the second example, 'we' makes it seem as if the speaker is part of a powerful group. The 'you' in that example directly addresses the audience, inviting them to consider their responses.

3   Write a 150-word analysis of the use, variation and impact of pronouns in Emma Watson's speech.

4   You are going to write a persuasive speech about a global issue you feel strongly about, such as the environment, disability or poverty.

Assume your audience is English-speaking adults around the world, so think carefully about appropriate content and formality. Use some of the techniques you identified in Activity 2, and choose pronouns carefully as part of your persuasive strategy.

Write approximately 400 words in standard English.

5   Edit your speech, then deliver it to the class, adapting your voice and gestures to have an impact on your audience. Use visual aids if appropriate.

> ### Writing tip
>
> Adult audiences are usually aware of the ways that speakers use to try to manipulate them, so be subtle in your use of persuasive techniques.

> ## Peer assessment
>
> Listen to other learners giving their speeches. As a class, share feedback on:
>
> - the effectiveness of the persuasive techniques used
>
> - the impact of any variations in communication.

> ## Summary checklist
>
> ☐ I can identify and comment on the techniques used in a persuasive speech.
>
> ☐ I can analyse the effects that different pronoun choices have on a reader or audience.
>
> ☐ I can write and deliver a persuasive speech for a specific audience, using appropriate techniques.

> 8.5 The transporter

In this session, you will:

- explore the features and effect of a futuristic story
- compare the presentation of young characters in two texts
- respond to different views about a story opening.

Getting started

In pairs, discuss the types of characters, settings and plots found in books and films that are set in the future. Do you enjoy this type of story? Why or why not?

Binti

The following extract is from *Binti*, a futuristic story by Nnedi Okorafor. Binti, an 18-year-old girl, is a member of the Himba people. She is the first Himba to be offered a place at Oomza University, far across the galaxy. The extract is about her leaving home.

Extract 1

I powered up the transporter and said a silent prayer. I had no idea what I was going to do if it didn't work. My transporter was cheap, so even a droplet of moisture, or more likely, a grain of sand, would cause it to **short**. It was faulty and most of the time I had to restart it over and over before if worked. Please not now, please not now, I thought.

The transporter shivered in the sand and I held my breath. Tiny, flat, and black as a prayer stone, it buzzed softly and then slowly rose from the sand. Finally, it produced the baggage-lifting force. I grinned. Now I could make it to the shuttle. 'Thank you,' I whispered. It was a half-mile walk along the dark desert road. With the transporter working, I would make it there on time.

Straightening up, I paused and shut my eyes. Now the weight of my entire life was pressing on my shoulders. I was defying the most traditional part of myself for the first time in my entire life. I was leaving in the dead of night and they had no clue. My nine siblings, all older than me except for my younger sister and brother, would never see this coming. My parents would never imagine I'd do such a thing in a million years. By the time they all realised what I'd done and where I was going, I'd have left the planet. In my absence, my parents would growl to each other that I was to never set foot in their home again. My four aunties and two uncles who lived down the road would shout and gossip among themselves about how I'd **scandalised our entire bloodline**. I was going to be a **pariah**.

'Go,' I softly whispered to the transporter, stamping my foot. The thin metal rings I wore around each ankle jingled noisily, but I stamped my foot again. Once on, the transporter worked best when I didn't touch it. 'Go,' I said again, sweat forming on my brow. When nothing moved, I chanced giving the two large suitcases sitting **atop** the force field a shove. They moved smoothly and I breathed another sigh of relief. At least some luck was on my side.

short: stop working; malfunction

scandalised our entire bloodline: brought shame on the whole family
pariah: an outcast
atop: on top of

1   Reread the extract.

    a   Note down the aspects of the story that seem unusual and those that seem normal or recognisable.

    b   With a partner, discuss the effect of this combination.

2   *Binti* and *I Want to Fly* both feature young characters who want a different type of life.

    Compare the way Binti's experience and Yinka's experiences in Extract 1 (Session 8.1) are presented. Using references from both texts, make notes on:

- how each character feels about their situation

- the attitude of their families

- whether you view them as sympathetic characters.

    Choose the best way to present your notes to ensure they are clear, as you will compare them with a partner and then use them to write an essay.

> **Writing tip**
>
> You can make notes in different ways, such as a spider diagram, a table or a bullet-point list. Choose the best option for the task. For example, a table might be more useful than a spider diagram if you are making notes under various headings.

Peer assessment

Swap notes with a partner and feed back on the following.

- Their note taking method – how useful is it for the task?

- The clarity of their note taking – is it legible and does it make sense?

---

3   Using your notes, write a comparison of the ways that the experiences of young people are presented in *Binti* and *I Want to Fly*. Write approximately 250 words.

4   Readers' opinions are often linked to their personal preferences. For example, someone may either really enjoy or strongly dislike historical texts or texts set in the future.

    Read the opinion on the next page about the opening of *Binti*. In pairs, discuss:

- this view of the story – what this learner thinks and what has influenced their response

- your own reactions to the setting and events in the extract.

> I thought this was a really good opening. I enjoy futuristic stories, because they include unusual gadgets and things we don't have in our real world. That's mainly what makes it exciting. The situation – leaving home and the pressures of teenage life – is a very normal one, but by putting it in a futuristic setting, it becomes much more interesting and shows that people's feelings and pressures are very similar no matter what time you live in.

5 Using your discussion from Activity 4, write a summary of the different views you have considered about the opening of *Binti*. Complete your summary with your own thoughts on how interesting you found it.

- How has your ability to respond to different opinions developed this year?
- How confident do you feel about giving and justifying your own views?

Summary checklist

- [ ] I can identify the features of a futuristic story and analyse their effects.
- [ ] I can compare the presentation of characters in two texts on similar themes.
- [ ] I can give a thoughtful response to different views about a story opening.

> 8.6 A strange ship

In this session, you will:

- explore how conflict, mystery and tension are created in fiction
- learn about the conventions of science fiction
- consider the functions of dialogue and narrator's voice
- write part of a futuristic story.

Getting started

What do you think are the differences and similarities between fantasy and science-fiction stories? Discuss your ideas in pairs.

Read the next extract from *Binti*, where she prepares to leave her planet.

Extract 2

The security guard **scowled** when I stepped forward. Behind him I could see three entrances, the one in the middle led into the ship called *Third Fish*, the ship I was to take to Oomza Uni. Its open door was large and round leading into a long corridor illuminated by soft blue lights.

'Step forward,' the guard said. I stepped forward and everything went red and warm.

When the body scan beeped its completion, the security guard reached right into my left pocket and brought out my **edan**. He held it to his face with a deep scowl.

I waited. What would he know?

He was inspecting its cube shape, pressing its many points with his finger and eyeing the strange symbols on it that I had spent two years unsuccessfully trying to decode. He held it to his face to better see the loops and swirls of blue and black and white.

> **scowled:** frowned in a bad-tempered way
> **edan:** a made-up word – a metal cube

'What is this made of?' the guard asked, holding it over a scanner. 'It's not reading as any known metal.'

I shrugged, too aware of the people behind me waiting in line and staring at me.

'Your identity reads that you're a harmonizer, a masterful one who builds some of the finest **astrolabes**,' he said. 'But this object isn't an astrolabe. Did you build it? And how can you build something and not know what it's made of?'

'I didn't build it,' I said.

'Who did?'

'It's . . . it's just an old, old thing that I carry for good luck.' This was partially a lie. But even I didn't know exactly what it could and couldn't do.

The man looked as if he would ask more, but didn't. Inside, I smiled. He had no idea, but he didn't want to show that I, a poor Himba girl, was more educated than he. So he quickly moved me along and, finally, there I stood at my ship's entrance.

The ship was a magnificent piece of living technology, a type of ship enhanced to grow three breathing chambers within their bodies.

Scientists planted rapidly growing plants within these three enormous rooms that produced oxygen from the CO_2 directed in from other parts of the ship. Once settled on the ship, I was determined to convince someone to let me see one of these amazing rooms. But at the moment, I wasn't thinking about the technology of the ship. I was on the **threshold** now, between home and my future.

astrolabe: a navigation device used on ships
threshold: a point between two rooms

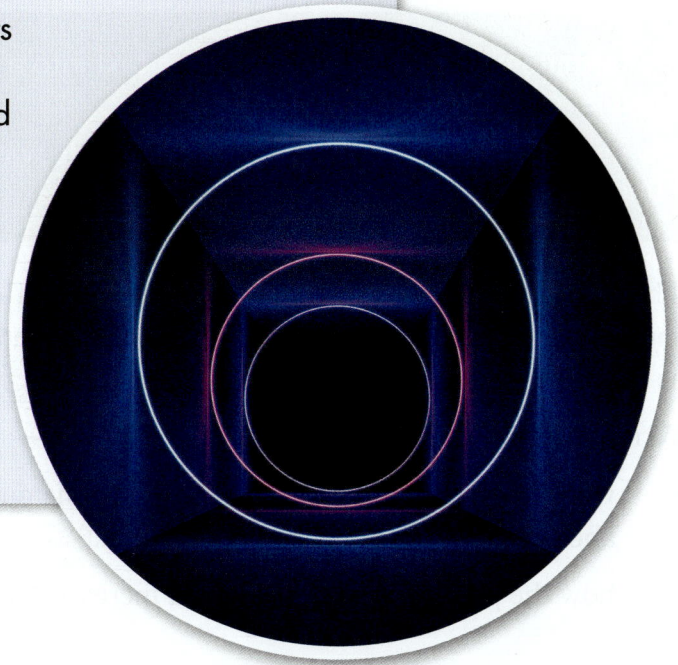

1   In pairs, discuss how effectively you think the writer creates conflict, mystery and tension in this extract. You could explore:

   • Binti's interaction with the security guard

   • the technology mentioned in the extract

   • any relevant uses of language.

2   Remember that the genre of science fiction uses ideas that are currently possible, or likely to happen in the future, while fantasy stories include ideas, objects and situations that are not possible in the real world.

   Here are some more features of science fiction:

   • plots involving travel through time and/or space

   • imaginary worlds

   • aliens or strange beings

   • unusual journeys

   • conflict between different types of beings

   • powerful technology.

   In pairs, discuss whether you would classify *Binti* as a science-fiction or a fantasy story. Use references from both extracts to support your ideas.

   • What are the challenges of classifying a text into a particular genre?

   • How useful have you found genre features as a way of understanding fiction?

3   This story is structured through a combination of dialogue and the narrator's voice. This gives the reader some details about Binti, as well as encouraging sympathy for her.

   Write two paragraphs explaining:

   • what the interaction between Binti and the guard reveals about her background and personality

   • how the presentation of the guard increases sympathy for Binti.

4   You are now going to write the next part of *Binti*. Remember that she:

- has a mysterious *edan* that she does not understand

- is travelling alone to a new life in a very unusual ship

- wants to see the amazing rooms on the ship.

Start by thinking about how you will develop the story. Remember that conflict, mystery and tension are essential parts of any plot, so experiment with the content and structure of your writing to see how you can create different effects.

Use voice and language appropriate to the story, perhaps inventing some names for futuristic devices. Write about 400 words.

> **Writing tip**
>
> When planning a plot, think about how you can 'move the story on'. For example, one way to do this is to introduce a new character who contrasts or conflicts with the central character.

Self-assessment

How effective is the structure and plot of your story? Consider how well you have:

- used conflict, mystery or tension to maintain the reader's interest

- developed the story – have you 'moved it on'?

Summary checklist

☐ I can analyse how a writer has created conflict, mystery and tension in a science-fiction extract.

☐ I understand the conventions of science-fiction writing.

☐ I can explain how dialogue and narrator's voice can be used to structure a story.

☐ I can continue a futuristic story, using appropriate voice, language and structural features.

Check your progress

Answer the following questions.

1   'Physical actions and symbols are important ways of telling stories in drama.' Using examples, explain what this statement means.

2   Explain the effects of using contrasting characters in a drama scene.

3   Using an example, explain the possible effects of retelling an account from different perspectives.

4   Explain the effect of different pronoun choices in persuasive texts.

5   'Choose the best form of note taking to suit the purpose.' Explain, using examples, what this statement means.

6   Summarise the features of science-fiction texts.

Project

Many texts feature privileged people, often those with status and authority such as celebrities and powerful people. In this unit you have read texts that feature different voices, such as young women living in poverty and people with disabilities.

In groups of four, you are going to produce an anthology of writing, featuring different or unusual voices and situations. For example, you could collect:

- feature articles and newspaper articles about people and groups who do not usually appear in the media

- interviews with people who have unusual backgrounds or particular disabilities

- poetry and plays by authors from a range of ethnicities

- stories featuring characters whose skills, abilities and backgrounds seem different to those who normally appear in fiction

- stories featuring 'outsiders' – those central characters who do not fit in with the society they live in.

Start by researching a range of fiction and non-fiction texts from some of the categories listed. Each group member should then:

* select one text to focus on

* copy a section from each text that is particularly interesting (300–400 words)

* write a 200-word account explaining why they have chosen the text, what it shows about the person or character featured, and why they would recommend the text.

Collect your work into a book or display to share with your class. Use the most appropriate layout to make it look as attractive and informative as possible.

9 > Strange and unusual

In this unit, you will study texts about strange feelings and occurrences. You will read a poem about a man who feels like a stranger in a new country, and explore the unusual events of Shakespeare's play *Macbeth*. You will read about space travel and analyse a science-fiction story with an unexpected ending.

> 9.1 Stranger in a strange land

In this session, you will:

- explore meaning in a poem
- consider the effect of language choices on meaning
- discuss the effect of structural choices in a poem.

Getting started

How would it feel to move to a different country? What might be enjoyable and what challenges might you face? Discuss your ideas in pairs.

'This Landscape, These People'

In the project at the end of the previous unit, you started to think about people who feel like strangers in the world they live in. In the poem 'This Landscape, These People', Zulfikar Ghose describes the experience of moving to England, having left India as a young man. In Extract 1, the poet describes walking through Putney Heath, an area in London. He feels like a stranger in his new country. He then thinks back to his childhood in India and why he left.

Extract 1

I

My eighth spring in England I walk among
   The silver birches of Putney Heath,
   Stepping over twigs and stones: being stranger,
   I see but do not touch: only the earth
   Permits an attachment. I do not wish
To be seen, and move, eyes at my sides, like a fish.

A child at a museum, England for me
   Is an **exhibit** within a glass case.
   The country, like an antique chair, has a rope
   Across it. I may not sit, only pace
   Its frontiers. I slip through ponds, jump ditches,
Through galleries of **ferns** see England in pictures.

II

My seventeen years in India, I swam
   Along the silver beaches of Bombay,
   Pulled coconuts from the sky and tramped
   Red horizons with the **swagger and sway**
   Of Romantic youth; with the **impudence**
Of a native tongue, I cried for independence.

Born to this continent, all was mine
   To pluck and taste: **pomegranates** to purple
   My tongue and chillies to burn my mouth. Stones
   Were there to kick. This landscape, these people –
   Bound by the rope and consumed by their own fire.
Born here, among these people, I was a stranger.

exhibit: an object on display
fern: a green plant
swagger and sway: confident, perhaps arrogant, movements
impudence: overconfidence; disrespectfulness
pomegranate: a fruit with red flesh

1 Complete the following tasks in pairs.

   a Work out the meanings of any unfamiliar words not mentioned in the glossary.

   b Note down lines that suggest the poet feels like a stranger in England.

   c Identify images of freedom connected with India.

   d Infer why the poet leaves India.

2 The writer uses language techniques to describe his relationship with both countries. Write an analysis of:

   • the similes in the second stanza

   • the images that appeal to the sense of taste in the fourth stanza.

Now read the final part of the poem, where the poet describes his current feelings towards England.

> **Reading tip**
>
> Remember that when analysing language, it is important to show detailed thinking. Consider all the connotations of the words used in any figurative language, and the range of possible interpretations.

Extract 2

III

Now I am **intimate**
   With England; we meet, secret as lovers.
   I pluck leaves and speak into the air's mouth;
   As a woman's hair, I **deck** with flowers
   The **willow's** branches; I sit by the pond,
My eyes are stars in its stillness; as with a wand,

I stir the water with a finger until
   It tosses waves, until countries appear
   From its dark bed: the road from Putney Hill
   Runs across oceans into the harbour
   Of Bombay. To this country I have come.
Stranger or an inhabitant, this is my home.

> **intimate:** familiar and relaxed
> **deck:** decorate
> **willow:** a tree growing near water

3 Write an analysis of Part III, explaining:

   • the poet's feelings towards England

   • the effect of figurative language

   • the effect of pastoral images.

Language focus

An ambiguous ending is one that is open to different interpretations. When ideas or events are left unresolved or uncertain, it can create an unsettling but powerful effect on the reader. For example, look at these final two sentences of a story:

- I looked across the water, and asked her to marry me. She was silent for a moment then uttered words I never expected to hear.

Did the woman accept the proposal or not? The reader does not know – but they are left intrigued! The reader can make up their own mind.

Ambiguous endings can also be used to suggest mixed feelings. For example:

- I packed my bags and closed the door quietly. My new life was beginning and my old one was ending.

In this example, the narrator does not confirm how they feel, which may suggest an inner conflict. The ending creates a bittersweet feeling, leaving the reader with a final impression of the narrator's uncertain situation.

4   In pairs, discuss the effect of the following structural features of the poem:

- the opening and closing stanzas that show differing views of the poet's feelings towards England

- the use of contrast in the middle section, which uses a flashback to life in India

- the use of rhyming couplets at the end of each stanza

- the ambiguity of the final couplet – in what different ways could you interpret this ending?

- How confident do you feel about analysing poetic structure?
- Has your confidence increased during your studies this year? If so, what helped?

> 9.2 A strange meeting

In this session, you will:

- explore language, plot and characterisation in an older play

- consider metaphorical meaning

- learn about the conventions of tragedy

- compare the plot and moral messages of two texts.

Getting started

In pairs, make a list of things you know or have heard about Shakespeare's play *Macbeth*. You could use this image from a graphic version of the play to make some guesses about plot and characters.

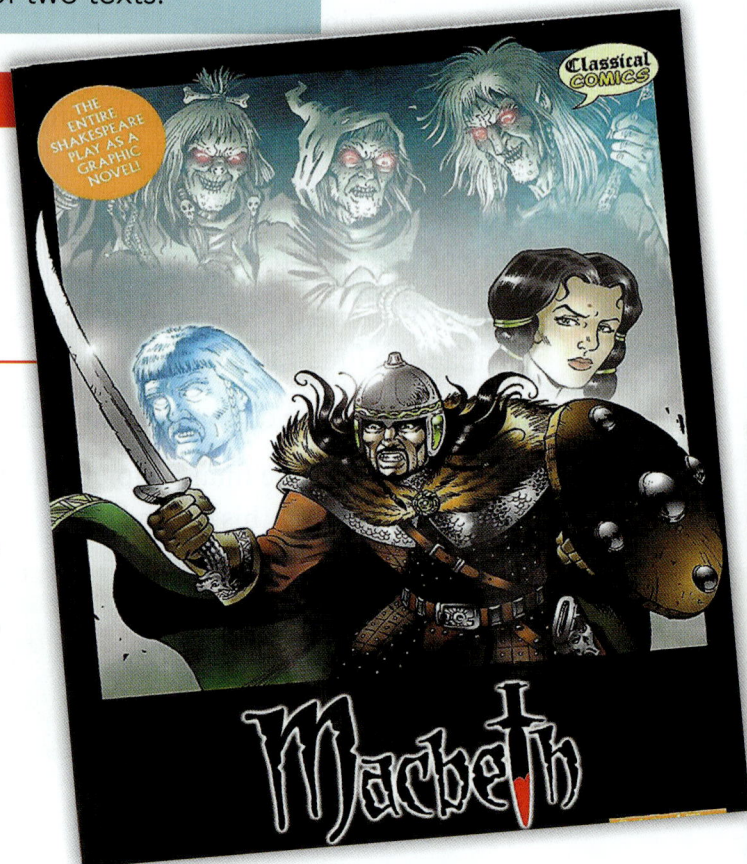

Macbeth

Macbeth is a play set in Scotland, about a man whose desire for power leads him to make terrible decisions. At the start of the play, we learn that:

- Macbeth is a brave and respected man

- he is a general in the army and is loyal to King Duncan

- he is Thane (ruler) of Glamis, an area of Scotland.

1   In the third scene of the play, Macbeth meets three strange characters – the weird sisters.

In groups of four, look at the image below then carry out the following tasks.

a   Discuss the way the four characters are presented – what does the image suggest about their power or status and personalities?

b   Read the speech bubbles, taking one part each.

c   Work together to write a translation in modern English.

hail: hello; an enthusiastic, respectful greeting
thee: you
Cawdor: an area of Scotland
shalt: shall
hereafter: in the future

Macbeth's meeting with the weird sisters is very mysterious. Although they greet him correctly as Thane of Glamis, they predict he will rule Cawdor too and also become king. In the next scene, Macbeth is made Thane of Cawdor by King Duncan. After this first prediction comes true, he is tempted to commit a terrible crime – killing the king in order to become king himself.

2 The five quotations below are said by Macbeth in his **soliloquy**, as he considers this crime. In pairs, match the quotation to its modern translation.

Key word

soliloquy: a solo speech in which a character reveals their thoughts

Reading tip

When trying to work out the meaning of phrases in Shakespeare's writing, remember that many of the expressions are figurative. Translate the literal meanings of words, but then 'stand back' from the translation to judge whether or not Shakespeare is using the phrase metaphorically.

Quotations

A If it were done when 'tis done, then 'twere well It were done quickly

B we but teach Bloody instructions, which, being taught, return To plague the inventor

C I am his kinsman and host, Who should against his murderer shut the door, Not bear the knife myself.

D this Duncan Hath borne his faculties so meek

E I have no spur To prick the sides of my intent, but only Vaulting ambition

Modern translations

i The king has performed his job in a gentle way.

ii It would be best for the murder to be done quickly.

iii The only reason I have to commit murder is ambition.

iv I should be protecting Duncan.

v People who murder others will suffer themselves.

3 Using the quotations from Activities 1 and 2, write a summary of the events of the play so far.

- Explain what has happened to Macbeth and how he has reacted to it.

- Comment on how Shakespeare uses metaphor to present Macbeth's thoughts.

- Say if you think Macbeth is an evil character.

Macbeth is encouraged to kill King Duncan by his wife, Lady Macbeth. He commits the crime and becomes king, but there are terrible consequences. Macbeth never experiences peace of mind or happiness again. Below is part of Macbeth's final soliloquy from the play, in which he talks about how pointless life is.

> And all our yesterdays have **lighted** fools
> The way to dusty death. Out, out, brief candle!
> Life's but a walking shadow, a poor **player**
> That **struts and frets** his hour upon the stage
> And then is heard no more: it is a tale
> Told by an idiot, full of sound and fury,
> **Signifying** nothing.

lighted: shown, lit the way to
player: actor
struts and frets: performs energetically
signifying: meaning

4 In this extract, Macbeth compares life to three things – a candle, an actor and a tale. Write an analysis of the three metaphors – what do they reveal about Macbeth's state of mind?

You could try reading the soliloquy out loud to help you understand how he might feel.

• What do you think are the main challenges of analysing an older text?

• What advice would you give to learners when working with unfamiliar language?

5 The genre of *Macbeth* is **tragedy**. You are going to listen to an audio recording that explains the conventions of tragedy.

a As you listen, make notes on the features of the genre.

b Use the notes to help you write a brief explanation of which features of tragedy you have seen so far in Macbeth.

6 In Unit 3, you read the mystery story 'The Red-Headed League'. In it, the villain (John Clay) was driven by greed – he wanted to take the bank's gold coins and he tricked Jabez Wilson in order to do it. His attempts at stealing were stopped, and he was caught and arrested.

Here is a summary of what happens in *Macbeth*:

• Macbeth is tempted by the weird sisters' predictions

• he kills King Duncan

• Macbeth commits other murders in order to keep power

• his friends and supporters do not trust him and desert him

• Lady Macbeth dies

• Macbeth is killed by a soldier loyal to King Duncan

• a new, rightful king takes charge.

In pairs, discuss:

• the similarities and differences between the narrative structure of 'The Red-Headed League' and *Macbeth*

• the moral messages that emerge from both stories.

> **Key word**
>
> tragedy: a genre of writing, especially drama, in which the main character encounters problems and suffering

---

Summary checklist

☐ I understand features of an older play, including language, plot and characterisation.

☐ I can explain how a playwright has used metaphor to reflect meaning.

☐ I understand the conventions of tragedy.

☐ I can compare the plot of two texts, including their moral messages.

> 9.3 Fun with **Macbeth**

In this session, you will:

- explore content and meaning in updated versions of *Macbeth*
- compare two different versions of the same story
- plan and write your own version of the play.

Getting started

How could you bring the story of *Macbeth* up to date? For example, how might it be turned into a science-fiction story? Discuss your ideas in pairs.

Macbeth in India

Macbeth has been produced on stage and in film many times. Some writers adapt the story into modern English and put it in a new setting. The next extract is from a review by N. Sudarshan in the *Deccan Herald* of a film version of *Macbeth* called *Paddayi*.

A poetic retelling of *Macbeth* in a new India

Paddayi is set in a beautiful coastal village. The story of Madhava and Sugandhi, the Macbeth couple, also encompasses the fishing community caught up in the whirlwind of a new economy and modernisation.

Madhava is part of a group of fishermen headed by Dineshanna who continues with traditional fishing using wooden boats while others practise aggressive methods to the **detriment** of the environment. Madhava is an able fisherman contributing to the wealth of Dineshanna while Sugandhi is drawn to the imported perfumes which only the rich can afford.

Poverty drives the ambition and greed of the couple thrusting them into a **hitherto inaccessible** new world. The recurring image of the fish gasping on the floor of the boat is one of the many such poetic reflections on Madhava's tragic situation.

1   Make notes on:

- what the new setting of the story is

- Madhava's and Sugandi's motivations that thrust them into an 'inaccessible new world'

- how the image of the fish could be interpreted as a symbol for tragedy.

> **detriment:** the state of being damaged or harmed
>
> **hitherto inaccessible:** could not be accessed or reached until now

'Call Me Mac'

The following extract is from a prose retelling of *Macbeth* by Humphrey Carpenter. It is written in the voice of an American private detective. The language and style of the story mimic the work of American writers from the 1940s and 1950s, such as Raymond Chandler. Chandler wrote detective fiction featuring tough central characters. The tone of 'Call Me Mac' is meant to be comic and the narrator deliberately makes the situation sound strange. Here, he describes meeting the weird sisters on the 'blasted heath' – a stormy open field.

<u>It was the kind of day when you can do your washing without taking your clothes off.</u> That's to say, damp.

Scotland's a big place, and we had most of it to cross to get back home. A lot of the scenery looks as though someone backstage is having a joke, and this bit was no exception. They called it a blasted heath. <u>It looked as if whoever drew it had been trying to rub it out ever since.</u> Kind of weird.

But not as weird as the three dames we ran into.

'Hail!' yelled out <u>the youngest of them, and she wouldn't see ninety-five again.</u> I looked up into the sky. Well, I thought she was talking about the weather!

'All hail, Macbeth!' screamed the second, <u>who'd passed her sell-by date a couple of centuries ago.</u> 'Hail, Thane of Cawdor.'

'You got the wrong guy, ladies', I told them. But they hadn't finished.

'All hail, Macbeth, who'll be king one day!' screamed <u>the third, who made the other two look like winners in a beautiful baby contest.</u>

This was ridiculous. <u>No one gets to be king unless he's got royal blood in his veins. Or unless he drains a bucketful of the stuff out of its rightful owners.</u>

2 In pairs:

    a work out what the underlined phrases mean

    b discuss what effect the informality of the narrator's tone has on the story.

3 Both texts you have read in this session retell *Macbeth* in different ways. Write a 250-word comparison of these two versions, explaining:

- the different attitude and values they show

- which one you prefer and why.

4 *Macbeth* is a very adaptable text – the basic story and ideas can be transferred into different settings, genres and times. Here are two examples of versions that have been filmed in recent years:

- a head chef in a successful restaurant does all the work, but the owner takes all the money

- the rich Chief Executive of a powerful oil company is envied by his ambitious deputy.

Write your own prose version of *Macbeth*. You should set it in a distinctive place and include a reason for him to seek power. Tell the story of his meeting with the weird sisters, his feelings about Duncan and his later suffering.

You will need to invent some details of your own. Start by deciding:

- where you will set the story

- whose point of view you will write from

- whether you will use a serious or comic voice.

Write 500 words. When you have finished your first draft, edit your work to check that your spelling, grammar and punctuation are accurate.

> **Reading tip**
>
> When trying to work out the underlying meanings of phrases, always think about the voice. Often, the narrator's tone and attitude will offer clues about whether the phrases are comic or sarcastic, for example.

> **Peer assessment**
>
> Swap work with a partner. Feed back on the effectiveness of the choices they have made.
>
> - Have they chosen an interesting setting for their story?
>
> - Have they used the basic plot details alongside some original and engaging new details?

› 9.4 An unusual job

In this session, you will:

- practise note taking and summarising skills based on an interview text

- discuss the effect of structural features in an article

- consider how representation is linked to readership and structural choices

- write a feature article for an adult audience.

Getting started

Science-fiction stories often feature space travel. If you were given a chance to train as an astronaut in real life, would you accept the challenge? Why or why not? Discuss your views in groups.

Interview with an astronaut

In Unit 8, you read *Binti*, a futuristic tale about space travel. In the real world, a very small group of people have had the unusual experience of space travel as part of their job. In 2015, Christina Koch was chosen out of 6000 applicants to complete astronaut training. She has university degrees in engineering and physics. Read the following interview with Koch by Kristen Bobst from *Teen Vogue*.

71

Interview with astronaut

Christina Koch

Teen Vogue: Who inspired you along your journey to become a **NASA** Astronaut?

Christina Koch: Outside of my family, I was always inspired by true heroic stories of leadership and survival. For example, the story of the Shackleton expedition, when their ship became **lodged** in the Antarctic ice pack while exploring.

TV: What was your favorite part of astronaut training?

CK: My favorite was spacewalk training. You get to wear a full spacesuit just like the ones they use in orbit. It is very physically demanding as well, so I loved the challenge of having to get super in-shape just to be ready to focus on learning the tools and skills needed for the spacewalk tasks.

TV: What's been your greatest challenge so far?

CK: Recently, I got to train to be an aircraft commander of another military high-performance plane called a T-6. It took every bit of **grit** and dedication to get through that course. Along with the challenge of learning skills like this is the every-day challenge of adapting to the wide range of new circumstances you encounter in this job.

TV: What will you eat in space? Are you looking forward to any particular space meal?

CK: There's a team of people that provide really good space food. We've gotten to try a lot of it and it's really good. I am looking forward to trying some of the Japanese space food too! I wish I could say I'll be eating astronaut ice cream, but that's actually not something that's on NASA's standard menu!

TV: If you could bring three people (non-astronauts) to space with you, who would you bring?

CK: My husband and my parents. My parents gave me everything I needed to chase my dreams. And my husband is my best friend.

TV: If you weren't an astronaut, what other profession would you be interested in?

CK: I love building and fixing things, and so I always **gravitated** toward engineering or science instrumentation work. It's a bonus if I get to do that work in an interesting place like in the Antarctic or a remote island. I also love community service, tutoring or anything that spreads the love of science or reading.

Note: this text uses American spellings.

NASA: National Aeronautics and Space Administration
lodged: stuck

grit: determination
gravitated: be attracted to

1 Make notes on Koch's experiences, views and feelings. Use the most appropriate strategy to locate and note down key information.

2 Use your notes to write a summary of Christina Koch, as if you were writing a brief online biography about her. Write about 100 words.

3 The interview with Christina Koch originally appeared in a magazine aimed at female teenagers. Magazines are usually intended as quick reads – a reader 'dips into' them rather than reading from start to finish. Articles tend to be brief and easy to read.

In pairs, discuss the structure of the article. Consider:

- why the writer might have organised it in question-and-answer format, rather than writing it up as a feature article

- the effect of presenting Christina in her own words, rather than **paraphrasing** them.

4 Non-fiction writers have to decide how they want to represent the people they are writing about. For example, in the interview with Christina Koch, the writer will have:

- decided the type and focus of the questions (and also what not to focus on)

- edited Koch's answers to cut out any less interesting parts

- edited out fillers and less fluent parts of her responses.

In small groups, hold a structured discussion about how Christina Koch is represented in the article. Explore the following questions:

a What overall image do you get of the astronaut? Describe her qualities and attitudes.

b How is the article designed to create a positive image of her?

c Why has the writer chosen to represent Koch in this way? How might the target audience of the magazine have influenced this decision?

Writing tip

Reducing information to key points is an important skill. One way to do this is to write a list of facts and details in order of importance. This should help you identify the most useful material. The information at the top of your list should be included in your summary.

Key word

paraphrasing: rewording something in a different way, usually to make it shorter or clearer

---

Reading tip

When thinking about representation, it can be useful to consider what is missing or avoided in a text. For example, when reading interviews, think about the types of questions and topics that are *not* asked, and how this can influence the way a reader interprets things.

Remember to use appropriate language to explore these complex areas, take turns and keep the discussion going.

5   You are going to write a feature article on Christina Koch. Your audience is adult readers and the purpose is to explain why she is a positive role model for younger women.

Assume that your readers have heard of Christina, but do not know much about her, so you will need to explain some of her background and achievements.

- Use direct quotations from the interview, alongside other information you find as part of your research and planning.

- Use organisational features such as a headline and subheadings.

- Write around 500 words in an appropriate voice.

Start by planning the structure of your article, and reading some feature articles to help you understand the text type and broaden the vocabulary and language you will use.

Self-assessment

Read your draft and check you have:
- used an interesting headline that indicates what the article is about
- written an opening paragraph likely to engage your readers
- given a clear explanation in relation to the purpose.

Summary checklist

- ☐ I can take accurate notes and summarise information for a specific purpose.
- ☐ I can participate in a group discussion to explore the structural features of a text.
- ☐ I understand how representation is linked to readership and structural choices.
- ☐ I can use appropriate language and organisational features to write a feature article for an adult audience.

> 9.5 Unusual endings

Getting started

What types of story endings do you prefer – ones where events and problems are fully resolved, or ones that are unusual, which surprise or shock you? Discuss your ideas in pairs.

Story endings

In Session 9.2, you considered the ending of *Macbeth*. This is a conventional ending – the villain in the story is defeated. In Session 9.1, you considered the ambiguous couplet at the end of 'This Landscape, These People' and the effect it created. Endings are often related to genre. If a reader expects a story to end in a particular way because stories of that genre usually do, writers normally meet those expectations. Read the three descriptions of stories on the next page.

The End.

Abiola

This is a tragic play set in Ethiopia. Abiola is the brother of Emperor Chidi, a powerful and well-liked ruler. Abiola is a loyal brother, but his advisers suggest that Abiola himself should be emperor. At first, Abiola ignores them, but he is gradually tempted by money and power. Abiola arranges to have his brother kidnapped and taken abroad. Abiola then becomes emperor.

The Night Raids

This is a detective story set in Ireland, and is part of a series featuring Jack Keys, a crime solver. A series of night-time bank robberies have taken place. Each one is bigger and more spectacular than the last. A huge amount of money has been lost and the police have no idea who is behind it. The Irish government has asked Jack Keys to help.

Darkparis

This is a fantasy story set below the streets of Paris. Louis, the central character, is a bored and lonely 17-year-old who meets an unusual girl, Relic. She introduces him to Darkparis, the strange world below the ground, where Louis meets the powerful and odd Doorkeeper. Louis undergoes a series of tests, but is not sure (at first) why he has been chosen.

1   In pairs, discuss:

   - different ways these three texts could end – suggest conventional and unconventional endings for each text
   - the different effects and messages that each ending would create.

Back to *Binti*

In Sessions 8.5 and 8.6, you read the start of *Binti*, in which the central character is leaving home to go to university on a distant planet. She is carrying a mysterious gadget called an *edan* and travelling on a strange ship. Conventionally, texts involving a journey where the central character has to overcome a series of challenges usually result in success and the central character becoming a 'hero'. However, writers may decide to create different effects by blending genres or providing unusual resolutions.

2   You are going to work in a group of three to explore different versions of *Binti*. Start by reading summaries A–C below and discussing your reactions to them. Consider:

  •   what the additional genre/unexpected elements contribute

  •   the ideas and values suggested in each version

  •   the different moral messages in each ending

  •   which ending you prefer and why.

A

Once Binti leaves the planet, the focus switches to her family. They are horrified to learn from a mysterious visitor that her *edan* is dangerous and is being sought by the Shari, a powerful criminal gang. The story becomes a race to find Binti between members of the Shari and Haro, Binti's brother. In the final scene, Haro finds Binti and uses the *edan* to defeat the gang.

B

The ship arrives in Ooma and Binti attends university. On the first day, she learns that rather than being a place of education, it is training learners for a conflict with the neighbouring planet, Alcentor. Binti is being prepared and trained to be the leader of Ooma. Her mission is to conquer Alcentor. At first, Binti is unsure, but by the final scene, she has become a powerful and feared leader who will do anything to retain power.

C

At the very last moment, Binti decides to return home to be with her family. They never realise that she was about to leave home and life carries on as before, but Binti becomes increasingly bitter. She feels she has missed her chance. As the years go by, Binti has a family of her own, but in some ways, her life among the Himba people is unfulfilling. In the final scene, Binti's daughter, Amiri, is offered a place at Ooma University.

3   In your group of three, assign one of these different endings to each group member. Then write the final scene as described in the summary. Use appropriate language and varied sentence structures for the effect you are trying to create. Write approximately 400 words.

Peer assessment

Read each others' stories and give feedback. Comment on the effectiveness of these things.

- Language and sentence choices – did they help to create the appropriate atmosphere?
- The final sentence – was it well-crafted and memorable?

In the published version of *Binti*, Ooma University is threatened by a race called the Meduse. Binti helps the professors and the Meduse to understand each other and live in harmony. This occurs partly because of Binti's ability to make friends with Okwu, one of the Meduse. In the final scene, Okwu reminds Binti of the importance of family.

Here is the last paragraph of the novel.

72 I sat in the silence of my room looking at my *edan* as I sent out a signal to my family with my astrolabe. Outside was dark and I looked into the sky, at the stars, knowing the pink one was home. The first to answer was my mother.

4   In pairs, discuss this ending. Consider:

- the effect of ending the novel with Binti contacting her family
- what is implied about Binti's development by the end of the story
- whether you enjoyed this conventional ending.

Summary checklist

☐ I can analyse the effects of unconventional endings.

☐ I can write an unconventional ending to a story to create an effect.

☐ I can read and discuss the implications of a conventional ending.

> # 9.6 A twist in the tail

In this session, you will:

- explore how a writer blends elements of different genres
- discuss meanings and predict an ending
- consider the effects of puns and double meanings
- write your own story with a surprise ending.

Getting started

'A twist in the tail' is a metaphor that is used to describe surprise endings in stories. In pairs, explain how this metaphor works and discuss any stories you have read that end in a surprising way.

'To Serve Man'

'To Serve Man' by Damon Knight is a short story that combines elements of science fiction, comedy and thriller stories – texts that involve fear, mystery and unsettling events. It also has a surprise ending.

The story is set on Earth, but it begins with the arrival of the Kanamit, a race from another planet who attend a meeting of the United Nations, an international organisation of different countries. The Kanamit look like a blend of human and animal.

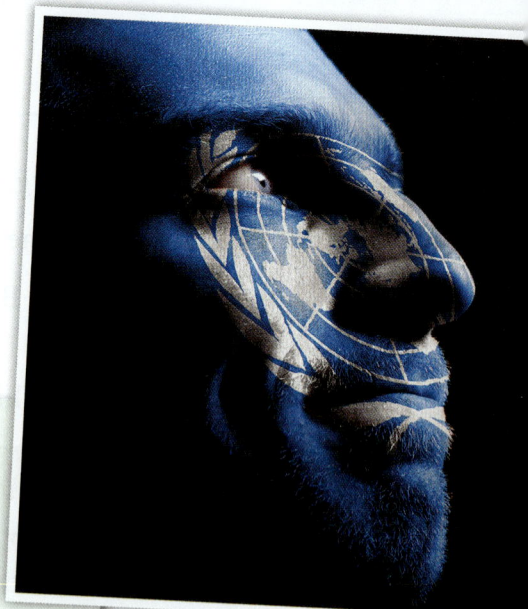

Extract 1

The Kanamit were not very pretty, it's true. Seeing them for the first time shocked you.

I don't know what we expected **interstellar** visitors to look like – those who thought about it at all, that is. Maybe that's why we were all so horrified and **repelled** when they landed in their great ships and we saw what they really were like.

There were three of them at this session of the U.N., and I can't tell you how queer it looked to see them there in the middle of a solemn session – three fat creatures in green **harnesses** and shorts, sitting at the long table, surrounded by delegates from every nation. They sat correctly upright, politely watching each speaker. Their flat ears drooped over the earphones. Later on, I believe, they learned every human language.

Note: this text uses American spellings.

> **interstellar:** between the stars, from space
> **repelled:** felt distaste
> **harnesses:** a set of straps

1   Write a paragraph analysing the effect of blending these genre elements, using examples from the text.

Many readers enjoy surprise endings, but it is important that a writer gives some clues throughout the text that this will happen and which make sense at the end. In the middle of 'To Serve Man', the writer gives a clue to the surprise ending by referring to the title of the story – which is the name of a book written by the Kanamit. The narrator and his friend spend a long time trying to interpret the Kanamit language. By this point in the story, humans trust the Kanamit and the changes they have made to human life.

Extract 2

We got the title worked out in a few weeks. It was *How to Serve Man*, evidently a handbook they were giving out to new Kanamit staff. They had new ones in, all the time now, a shipload about once a month; they were opening all kinds of research laboratories, clinics and so on.

It was astonishing to see the changes that had been wrought in less than a year. There were no more armies, no more shortages, no unemployment. When you picked up a newspaper the news was always good. The Kanamit were nearly ready to announce methods of making our race taller and stronger and healthier – practically a race of supermen – and they had a potential cure for disease.

2 In pairs, discuss:

- what the title of the book suggests about the Kanamit's attitude to humans and how this is supported by their actions

- what the surprise ending might be.

Language focus

Many words in English have more than one meaning. For example, the word 'leaves' is a verb meaning 'departs', but it is also a noun for the green growths on plants and trees. The context of a sentence usually makes it clear which meaning a writer intends, but sometimes writers play on these double meanings to create jokes or **puns** for comic effect. For example, this pun relies on the two meanings of the word 'struck':

- He was trying to remember what caused lightning when it suddenly struck him.

Here, one sense of 'struck' means 'to suddenly realise', and the other means 'to be hit'. Both of these meanings work in the context of the sentence and create a light humour. Scenes or even whole stories can be based on a character misunderstanding the meaning of a word. The effect is often comic but writers can also use wordplay for tragic or other effects.

Key word

pun: a type of wordplay that relies on a word with two meanings

Read the last paragraph of 'To Serve Man'. In it, the narrator's friend has finally worked out the meaning of the book title.

> **Extract 3**
>
> 'And the book?' I demanded, annoyed. 'What about that – *How to Serve Man*? That wasn't put there for you to read. They *mean* it. How do you explain that?'
>
> 'I've read the first paragraph of that book,' he said. 'Why do you suppose I haven't slept for a week?'
>
> I said, 'Well?' and he smiled a curious, twisted smile.
>
> 'It's a cookbook,' he said.

3   Write an analysis of the ending, exploring:

- the pun used in the title of the Kanamit's book

- the different ways that readers might react to this surprise ending: is this a funny joke, a criticism of human stupidity or a repulsive story?

- how you react to it.

Your final challenge

4   For your last writing task, you are going to write a short story with a surprise ending. It should be around 750 words and can be in a genre of your choice.

Use this piece of writing to show the progress you have made this year, taking care with language, sentence and structural choices that help to contribute to the overall effect you wish to create.

Remember to include 'clues' in the story to prepare the reader for the surprise.

Writing tip

When planning a surprise ending, think very carefully about the clues you use and where you place them. You will have to judge the extent of the information you give – make sure your clues do not give away the ending!

Peer assessment

Read your partner's story and give them some feedback on the following.

- The ending – did it comes as a surprise?
- The clues in the story – were they used and placed effectively?

Think about your progress during the year.
- What skills have you developed?
- Which piece of work are you most proud of?

Summary checklist

- ☐ I can analyse a story that blends different genre elements.
- ☐ I can understand the structure of a story with a surprise ending.
- ☐ I can comment on the effects of puns and double meanings.
- ☐ I can write a story with a surprise ending.

Check your progress

Answer the following questions.

1   'Readers come to expect conventional endings where problems are resolved, but when endings are "open" and left unresolved, the effect can be powerful.' Using an example, explain what this statement means.

2   Summarise the features of the genre of tragedy.

3   Give an example of a modern version of *Macbeth* and explain the effects of modernising the play.

4   'Writers of non-fiction also make key decisions about how they represent real people.' Using examples, explain what this statement means.

5   Give an account of conventional and unconventional endings in texts you have read and summarise the different effects created.

6   Give some tips for writing a story with a surprise ending. Use an example in your advice.

Project

In groups, you are going to design a new learning session on a topic of your choice.

During the course of this book, you will have noticed that each session is based around a theme and contains a text extract of 300–450 words followed by four or five learning activities. The activities are a mixture of reading, writing and speaking activities and mainly invite you to:

*   explore meanings and ideas in a text

*   discuss your own and other learners' reactions

*   analyse how language and structure are used

*   write an imaginative response

*   read or perform a text.

Plan and write a new session aimed at Stage 9 learners that contains *some* of the activity types listed above. Start by choosing a theme. Some of the themes we nearly used in this book were 'Wild animals', 'Help!' and 'Deep feelings'. You could use one of these themes or a new idea of your own. Next, find a text that will appeal to your readers and then discuss the activities you could include. Use language appropriate to your audience and ensure that your text is proofread and edited accurately.

Your session should be around 1000 words and presented in an appealing way. Choose two suitable pictures to accompany the text. Remember to take up group roles as appropriate.

> Glossary

> Acknowledgements

The author and publisher acknowledge the following sources of copyright material and are grateful for the permissions granted. While every effort has been made, it has not always been possible to identify the sources of all the material used, or to trace all copyright holders. If any omissions are brought to our notice, we will be happy to include the appropriate acknowledgements on reprinting.

Unit 2 'Confessions of an art detective' by Joseph Bullmore in the Gentleman's Journal. Used with permission of the author; abridged extract from *The Case of the Missing Masterpiece* by Terrance Dicks. Reproduced by permission of The Agency (London) Ltd © Terrance Dicks 1978. First published 1978 by Blackie and Sons Ltd, Piccolo edition published 1980 by Pan Books Ltd, Scholastic Publications Ltd edition first published 1980, All rights reserved and enquiries to The Agency (London) Ltd, 24 Pottery Lane, London W11 4LZ info@theagency. co.uk; **Unit 4:** 'Autumn', 'The Turning Year', 'The End of The Year' By Kenneth Rexroth, from the original by Su Tung P'o, from *One Hundred Poems From The Chinese*, copyright ©1971 by Kenneth Rexroth. Reprinted by permission of New Directions Publishing Corp.; 'Outside world still a mystery to tribe that time forgot' from The Scotsman, 28 Nov 2008, ©JPI Media Publishing Limited 2008; abridged extracts from *Tanglewreck* © Jeanette Winterson, 2008, Bloomsbury Publishing Plc. Reproduced by permission of Bloomsbury Publishing Plc. **Unit 5:** abridged extract from *Small Island* (stage version) by Andrea Levy adapted by Helen Edmundson, NHB Modern Plays, 2019. Reproduced by permission of Nick Hern Books; abridged Prologue from *The Boy Who Harnessed The Wind: Young Readers Edition* by William Kamkwamba and Bryan Mealer, text copyright © 2015 by William Kamkwamba and Bryan Mealer. Used by permission of Dial Books for Young Readers, an imprint of Penguin Young Readers Group, a division of Penguin Random House LLC. All rights reserved; 'A glimpse into K-pop idol wannabe's life' By Dong Sun-hwa, 29-07-2019 in the Korea Times. Reproduced by permission of Korea Times; 'Why zoos are good' by Dave Hone, 19 Aug 2014 Copyright Guardian News & Media Ltd 2020. Reproduced by permission of Guardian News & Media Ltd.; **Unit 6:** abridged extract from *If Nobody Speaks of Remarkable Things* by Jon McGregor, Reproduced by permission of Houghton Mifflin Harcourt; 'A Love Letter to the Grand Canyon' by James Kaiser, first published at www.oars.com, used with kind permission of the author; 'Vermont' by Phillip Whidden, *Encyclopedia Sonnetica*, phillipwhidden.com, used by kind permission of the author; **Unit 7:** 'The Journey Within' by Annelise Heurtier, abridged and used by kind permission of the author (translation © Sam Gordon, 2017), this translation first appeared in the anthology *Quest: Stories of Journeys from Around Europe from the Aarhus 39*, Alma Books; **Unit 8:** 'I Want to Fly' © Thembelihle Moyo, 2019, from *Contemporary Plays by African Women*, Bloomsbury Publishing Plc. Reproduced by permission of Bloomsbury Publishing Plc; Edited extract from "Just Crash Through it …" by Rosaleen Moriarty-Simmonds OBE, first published in 2005, for further reading see Rosaleen's autobiography: *Four Fingers and Thirteen Toes* – ISBN - 9781438942995.Used with permission of the author; 'Gender equality is your issue too' by Emma Watson, September 20, 2014, www.unwomen.org; abridged extract from *Binti*, by Nnedi Okorafor, Tom Doherty Associates, LLC, 2015; **Unit 9:** 'This Landscape, These People' from *The Loss of India* by Zulfikar Ghose © Zulfikar Ghose 1964. Reproduced by permission of Sheil Land Associates Ltd; Review of film Paddayi from 'A poetic retelling of Macbeth in a new India' by N Sudarshan, July 13 2018, Deccan Herald; abridged extract from 'Call Me Mac', in *Shakespeare without the Boring Bits*, Humphrey Carpenter, 1994. Reproduced by permission of Cecily Ware Literary Agents; *Macbeth: The Graphic Novel*, Classical Comics 2008. Reproduced with permission of Classical Comics; 'Interview with Astronaut Christina Koch' in Teen Vogue by Kristen Bobst, Sept 27, 2017; *To Serve Man* by Damon Knight, 1950. Used with permission of InfinityBox Press LLC on behalf of the author.

Thanks to the following for permission to reproduce images:

Cover image created by Justin Rowe; *Inside* Unit 1 Warren Weinstein/GI; DigiPub/GI; Sean Gladwell/GI; D-Keine/GI; Pengcen Xie/GI; Georgeclerk/GI; BJI/Blue Jean Images/GI; Shaunl/GI; Ands456/GI; Where Shadows Shrink/500px/GI; Felix Cesare/GI; John W Banagan/GI; Walter Bibikow/GI; Frans Lemmens/GI; Peter Field/500px/GI; Unit 2 Andrew Brookes/GI; AJ_Watt/GI; Digital Vision/GI; Peter Dazeley/GI; Daniel Allan/GI; Jan Hennop/GI; DrAfter123/GI; Peter Dazeley/GI; UpperCut Images/GI; Westend61/GI; Maciej Toporowicz NYC/GI; Tirc83/GI; Sean Gladwell/GI; Jeff Blackler/Shutterstock; South_agency/GI; Unit 3 Hartswood Films/BBC Wales/Album/Alamy; Album/British Library/Alamy; All Star Picture Library/Warner Bros./Alamy; Dougal Waters/GI; Photograph by Devon OpdenDries/GI; Eli_asenova/GI; Unit 4 Bruce Rolff/Stocktrek Images/GI; Hiromi Okada/GI; Pawel Libera/GI; MediaProduction/GI; Hello Africa/GI; Ulet Ifansasti/GI; Ulet Ifansasti/GI; Joe daniel price/GI; Ultraforma/GI; Tara Moore/GI; Tetra Images/GI; FredFroese/GI; Andrew Brookes/GI; Sciepro/Science Photo Library/GI; Klaus Vedfelt/GI; Unit 5 Jansos/Alamy; Daily Herald Archive/SSPL/GI; Leah Harvey in Small Island photo by Brinkhoff-Moegenburg; Topical Press Agency/GI; Lucas Oleniuk/Toronto Star/GI; Lifestyle pictures/Alamy; The Chosunilbo JNS/Imazins/GI; The Chosunilbo JNS/Imazins/GI; Ashraf Shazly/AFP/GI; Jan Kopec/GI; SasinT Gallery/GI; James Ennis/GI; Jordan Lye/GI; Hillary Kladke/GI; SolStock/GI; Unit 6 Pakin Songmor/GI; Dominic Meily/GI; Stephen Yelverton Photography/GI; FilippoBacci/GI; © Marco Bottigelli/GI; Peter Unger/GI; Ihlow/ullstein/GI; Werner Forman/Universal Images Group/GI; sharply_done/GI; Ron and Patty Thomas/GI; Jake Wyman/GI; Artur Debat/GI; Martyn Ferry/GI; Ryan McVay/GI; Rob DeCamp Photography/GI; Unit 7 Artur Debat/GI; Coneyl Jay/GI; Unit 8 RapidEye/GI; Image Source/GI; Denny Allen/GI; Klaus Vedfelt/GI; Martin-dm/GI; NickyLloyd/GI; Trevor Williams/GI; Copyright Rosaleen Moriarty Simmons. Used with permission of the author; Mark J Sullivan/Pacific Press/LightRocket/GI; LaylaBird/GI; Westend61/GI; Stocktrek Images/Kevin Lafin/GI; Colin Anderson Productions pty ltd/GI; Jorg Greuel/GI; kali9/GI; RubberBall Productions/GI; Unit 9 Gina Pricope/GI; Anand purohit/GI; Marcia Straub/GI; Robbie Jack/GI; PhotoStock-Israel/GI; Peepo/GI; Kirill Kudryavtsev/GI; Alexander Ryumin/TASS/GI; Nora Carol Photography/GI; cemagraphics/GI; Zoonar/Makarov Alexander/Alamy; Anton Petrus/GI; Yuri_Arcurs/GI

Key: GI= Getty Images.

The author would like to thank the following people for their support: Sarah Elsdon, Florence Kemsley, Sonya Newland, Rosalyn Scott, Naomi Sklar.